AUTHORITY AND THE RENEWAL OF AMERICAN THEOLOGY

AUTHORITY
AND THE
RENEWAL
OF
AMERICAN
THEOLOGY

DENNIS M. CAMPBELL

A PILGRIM PRESS BOOK
FROM
UNITED CHURCH PRESS

Library of Congress Cataloging in Publication Data
Campbell, Dennis M   1945-
  Authority and the renewal of American theology.

  "A Pilgrim Press book."
  Originally presented as the author's thesis, Duke, 1973.
  Bibliography: p.
    1.   Authority (Religion)—History of doctrines.
  2.   Theology, Doctrinal—History—United States.
  I.   Title.
BT88.C247 1976   230   75-40340
  ISBN 0-8298-0303-3

Excerpts from *Liberation Theology* by Frederick Herzog are © 1973 by Frederick Herzog. Reprinted by permission of the publisher, The Seabury Press, Inc.

United Church Press, 1505 Race Street, Philadelphia, Pennsylvania 19102

CONTENTS

PREFACE

The Christian church today is characterized by a decided effort to recover a sense of stability and clarity of purpose. We have come through more than a decade of serious questions about the role of the church in the modern world. Widely divergent alternatives ranging from the "death of God" to a resurgence of evangelical theology have been featured prominently in the news media, and a variety of polarizations within the church have been used to demonstrate all manner of hypotheses. Now the "big news" is the effort on the part of some Christians to reassert that there are foundations to the Christian faith and that these foundations—rightly understood—actually aid the mission of the whole church by emphasizing the vitality of the faith rather than the peculiarity of particular interpretations of the faith. As a Christian theologian, a minister and teacher, I have observed in study, parish, and classroom the need for a new approach to authority for theology and religious ethics.

My interest in the problem of authority for constructive theology and ethical reflection began in the course of an independent study project undertaken with Prof. James M. Gustafson while I was a student in Yale University Divinity School. My study convinced me that one might gain important understanding of a particular theological system and its implications for ethical prescription by attending to the authority which informs a theologian's writing. For several years I have brought the question of authority to my work in historical and contemporary theology. The present study is an effort to demonstrate the way in which critical examination of the concept "authority" may aid theological scholarship.

My research has been done primarily in the divinity school libraries of Duke and Yale universities. Jane E. McFarland, then reference librarian at Yale, greatly aided my initial work. Prof. Donn Michael Farris, librarian, and Harriet V. Leonard, reference librarian of the

Duke Divinity School Library, have been generous with their knowledge of the superb collections in the Divinity School Library and the William R. Perkins Library at Duke.

While in process, this study has been read in whole or in part by Profs. Stuart C. Henry, Irving B. Holley, Jr., Robert T. Osborn, James M. Gustafson, Henry B. Clark, Waldo Beach, and H. Shelton Smith. Special mention should be made of Prof. Thomas A. Langford, friend and teacher, who, despite his extraordinarily demanding schedule as Dean of the Divinity School at Duke, has given many hours to this project. To each of these persons I am truly thankful; both content and style of this book have benefited from their combined experience and evident interest.

I am indebted to Alfreda Kaplan, who typed the original manuscript, and to Vicki Hawkins, who completed the final manuscript. Shirley O'Neal came to my aid numerous times, and Clara Godwin consistently offered many kindnesses which made my work easier. Parishioners at Trinity United Methodist Church, Durham, North Carolina, and students at Duke Divinity School and Converse College have contributed more to this study than they could possibly know. The Rev. William K. Quick, special friend and ministerial colleague, offered valuable insight into the practical implications of the theoretical reflection.

Those who know me well know how important my wife, Leesa, has been to this project; all ought to know. Her own theological training has made her an indispensable initial critic; but most of all, she is an unfailing joy in total life and always makes my spirits soar.

DMC

INTRODUCTION

The protean character of contemporary American culture has produced a noticeable interest in the idea of authority. In the midst of intellectual and social disorganization, some persons clamor for stability and order; others celebrate the creative potential of flux and uncertainty. Discussions of authority cover a vast range of issues, areas of life, and fields of study. The concept "authority" is widely used, variously defined, and little understood. This study is intended to demonstrate one method of doing a careful analysis of the meaning of this complex issue and a sustained assessment of its significance for theology.

The term "authority" is most frequently used in one of four ways. In a political context, authority refers to various functioning agencies of *government*. These might be in any one of numerous forms, from monarchy to military dictatorships to democratic processes. In this use of the word would be included agencies as varied as a city police department, the New York Port Authority, or the governor of North Carolina. Moreover, these several forms of authority might be legitimated in any number of ways from raw force to moral suasion, depending on particular settings and systems. Political and social theorists differ widely in their analyses of this usage of "authority." The point to be made here is only that their reference is to variable forms of ordering common political groupings.[1]

Ideas, traditions, or *precedents* which are self-sustaining or sustained by communities constitute a second use of the word "authority." More subtle than legal or governmental authority, this second form of authority may or may not include the sanction of coercion. Family order is one example of this kind of authority; school traditions or monogamy in Western societies might be others.

A third major use of "authority" is with reference to a *personal characteristic*. Some persons are recognized as innately authoritative;

1

this natural ability to attract the support of others might be called charisma.[2] In this sense, a political leader may have legitimate authority to govern but may lack charismatic authority; similarly, one who has no official status of any sort but still elicits widespread respect, obedience, or compliance may be recognized as one who has "authority."[3]

Each of the first three uses of "authority" has reference to a particular reality which can be observed and described, a reality which is sufficiently compelling to bring about actions or beliefs on the part of individual persons or groups of people. A fourth use of "authority" has to do with means of legitimating methods of justifying claims. Here "authority" functions to describe operative procedures, or norms, for any number of social or intellectual processes. This use of "authority" is the broadest and most theoretical understanding of the word; it is also the most important use because it has reference to all aspects of life, including the uses of "authority" already described. Thus one might ask by what *authority* democratic authority is legitimated, or by what *authority* a charismatic leader is judged, or by what *authority* a doctor's judgment about drug use is rendered. Authority has by no means vanished from the modern world, but functions daily in many ways. Authority may be unarticulated, but social and intellectual aspects of both private and corporate life depend on a variety of authorities.

The fourth sense of the concept "authority," as it has here been described, is the one which applies to theology. This is not to be confused with the occasional use of the term to refer to ultimate authority, or God. Christianity has maintained that, apart from the myriad authorities of earthly existence, there is one authority which is final. The problem is that this authority can only be pointed to by men, never grasped; therefore, Christians have talked about *mediate authorities,* the fourth sense of the word, by which something may be known about ultimate authority.

Mediate authorities have to do with justification of choices among competing claims: Which critical tool, in other words, will be used to adjudicate among conflicting theological positions in the process of constructive theological formulation? Critical tools for Christianity have usually been the Bible, inner experience, church tradition, or creedal affirmation. Christian theology usually has recognized one, all, or any combination of these as functionally authoritative. Sometimes such things as secular philosophy, political persuasion, nationalism, or racial prejudice have been authoritative for theology. The nature of the particular mediate authority shapes the character of the entire theological construction.

Two factors make the problem of authority for theology particularly important. The first is that Christian faith has claimed to have unique insight into ultimate reality. Such a stance requires that mediate authority be taken with profound seriousness. The second grows naturally out of the first. Christianity has claimed to articulate authoritatively the meaning of ultimacy for the life and actions of individual persons and persons in community. Theology thus involves ethical prescription—of some sort—for the ordering of human life.

While theological authority is a primary issue, its nature has always been a source of debate. Ultimate authority has readily, or tacitly, been ascribed to God, but Christianity has never been of one mind with regard to mediate authority for theological thought and ethical prescription. Certain traditions have been prone to emphasize the scriptures; others, church tradition or inner experience; and still others, reason. The development of sophisticated methods of scientific and historical criticism in the nineteenth century challenged these norms by proposing to explain them in psychological, sociological, or historical terms; this resulted in an effort to find new norms for theology which would satisfy modern consciousness. The gradual growth of a predominantly secular culture has created a climate in which challenges to the validity of all norms are raised and has thus made the question of theological authority even more urgent.

The concept of authority, when it is used to refer to specific methodological procedures of constructive theology, is useful as an analytical tool for understanding theological systems. Examination of theology with reference to the question of authority demonstrates that, although theologians may not give specific attention to authority, they do not, and cannot, avoid using some functional authority for their work. These norms may be unarticulated and unexamined but they are not absent, and they are a basic consideration in interpreting and evaluating a theological effort.

The intention of this study is to demonstrate the way in which attention to the question of authority illuminates the study of theology. I have chosen to focus my work upon American thinkers in the context of the American experience. This method requires a careful study of complex historical developments in theology written in America. It has the advantage of testing the abstract concept of authority in the laboratory of history, using actual samples of the practice of theology. The plan, then, is to study the history of the problem of authority in American theology from the colonial period to the present and to suggest that such a study provides valuable insight for contemporary efforts at constructive theology.

I have selected five periods in American theology and have represented them with particular theologians, out of the conviction that the effectiveness of this study would depend on a detailed examination of authority in specific writers. The choice of Jonathan Edwards, Horace Bushnell, William Adams Brown, and H. Richard Niebuhr was based on several criteria. The first is the period in which they wrote; a history of authority will need to demonstrate adjustments in the nature of the problem of authority which have taken place as social and intellectual climates have changed. The second has to do with my judgment of their significance. Each of the men selected understood himself as a theologian, sought to explicate his thinking in a clear and original manner, and exerted great influence on theology through writings, lectures, or teaching. A third reason for my choice is that each sought to revitalize theology and, in doing this, offered a conception of authority for theological construction appropriate to changed social conditions and new intellectual realities.

In considering the fifth period, the present, I have identified four major theological positions in the contemporary United States and have selected representatives of these positions for particular attention. Careful review is given to the work of Langdon Gilkey, John B. Cobb, Jr., Gordon D. Kaufman, and liberation theologians, in particular, Frederick Herzog. Others might have been chosen, but these four, like the historical figures considered, understand themselves as theologians, are intellectually rigorous, and take their contemporary setting seriously while never overlooking the tradition in which they stand. The question put to their work is the same as that put to each of the historical figures: What exactly functions authoritatively for theology?

The test of the whole effort is whether or not there is a payoff for contemporary Christian theology. My contention is that the implications of the history of authority for the future of theology are great and that a renewal of theology in America will be the result of careful attention to the critical problem of authority. I have sought, in this book, to offer guidelines for just such a renewal.

CHAPTER I

AUTHORITY AND THE SENSE OF THE HEART: JONATHAN EDWARDS

1

RELIGIOUS VITALITY AND AUTHORITY IN A CHANGING SOCIAL ORDER

The precise nature of the Puritan church's role in colonial America has been susceptible to divergent interpretations. Some scholars have argued that the clergy literally ran the society in a decided rule of the priesthood, while others have maintained that the pious civil magistrates always held the upper hand. The complex issue of actual political control, however, should never be allowed to obscure the essential truth that religion and religious values were supremely important to the Puritan colonists. The church occupied a preeminent position in New England because it symbolically captured the meaning of the Puritans' wilderness venture into the untried future of America; it served to explain and buttress the entire order.

The Calvinist theology which undergirded Puritan thinking provided a picture of a fundamentally ordered universe. Though the English Puritans who came to America were by no means slavish adherents to the unyielding Calvinism of the *Institutes*, the Calvinist sense of order and authority remained intact. Every individual had a contribution to make to the smooth functioning of the whole society. Men and women were called to roles of diverse responsibility, but the ultimate authority was God alone. Transcendent authority translated into a hierarchy on earth in which ministers in the church community, magistrates in the civil community, and fathers in the familial community held their authority directly from God. Order was secure because it was understood that a challenge to familial, magisterial, or ministerial authority was in danger of upsetting the proper order of all creation, which was ordained by God.

In colonial New England, government consisted of a juxtaposition of multiple institutions, each of which had its place within the theological understanding of creation. There was no need for uncertainty or anxiety among Puritans as to the meaning of individual or corporate existence. Life was meaningful as part of an ordered whole in which authority was ordained and legitimated. As Perry Miller observed, "The great ecclesiastical discourses of the founders—Richard Mather's, John Cotton's, and above all Hooker's—set the system within a vast metaphysical, or rather cosmological, frame."[1] Religious and political authority were practically and theologically intermeshed.

Despite the important role the church played in society, however, its vitality began to wane, along with genuine enthusiasm for the holy experiment, shortly after initial colonization. Long before the end of the seventeenth century, the bright light of the Puritan religious mission was dimming. Perhaps this was a function of human nature—it is difficult to sustain fervent commitment over long periods of time—but certainly it was a function of human biology. Succeeding generations, born in America, did not share the enthusiasm for religion and the church which informed the early fathers when they arrived from England.[2]

The ratio of church members to the general population declined rapidly after 1652.[3] The reasons for the decline were many. Clearly the growth of a middle class and increasing wealth made Puritan religious activity less popular, but so did the sense of reasonable enlightenment which emerged out of education and exposure to primitive scientific experimentation. Religious belief and practice, which had been the dominant force in the lives of the early settlers, was not absent in late seventeenth-century New England, but it was not the all-consuming passion it once had been.

As religion became increasingly devoid of vitality, conviction about the theological meaning of life became less certain. Widespread was a feeling of guilt that the grand experiment of the forefathers had failed.[4] Clergy assailed the people; God did indeed have a controversy with his chosen. The theme, like the religion of which it was a part, became stereotyped: If the colonists would return to the godly ways of the fathers, then all would be well for the commonwealth. Theological reflection, mainly in the form of sermons, was largely limited to rehearsals of the former vitality of the true religion of New England. Recovery of theoretical and practical theology, however, was not destined to come out of admonitions to recreate the past but out of a new sense of the immediate reality of God.

Scattered stirrings of religious revival were reported in the late

6

seventeenth century. Solomon Stoddard, the great church leader of the Connecticut River valley, was visited by several quickenings of the spirit, which he called "harvests," in his Northampton congregation between the years 1680 and 1719. During 1733 and 1734, Jonathan Edwards led awakenings in Northampton and other communities along the Connecticut River. Theodore Frelinghuysen and William and Gilbert Tennent caused considerable notice when they came into New England from New Jersey to preach numerous revivals. The dam burst in 1740, however, with the arrival in New England of itinerant evangelist George Whitefield. The cities and rural areas alike were suddenly ablaze with religious passion. Historical interpretations vary, but of the reality of the revival phenomenon and the varied reactions to it there can be no doubt.

Throughout the colonies, the Awakening produced a severe conflict over the nature of religious authority and the implications of authority both for the attempt to describe the theological meaning of individual and corporate life and for the practical ordering of everyday existence. The evangelists of the Awakening taught that men might realize a direct, personal relationship with God. If God's authority could be thus immediately real for the individual, did this not threaten to undercut the traditional hierarchical patterns which invested clergy and civil magistrates with divinely sanctioned authority for the good of both religious order and social order?

Conservatives immediately recognized the revolutionary potential of the revivalist preaching. Their worst fears were vindicated when emotionally "awakened" colonists began to question the regeneracy of the clergy. The Harvard faculty, though it first welcomed Whitefield, soon changed its tune when his journal openly suggested that the college's "Light is become darkness."[5] The spirit of the revival threatened the establishment. The Harvard scholars condemned not only Whitefield but other itinerants who, following the Englishman's example, "thrust themselves into towns and parishes" and openly questioned the spiritual state of resident ministers, thereby working "to the destruction of all peace and order. " The people, the august faculty declared, infected with wrong ideas, might then "despise their own ministers" and refuse to recognize them as authorities.[6]

Arrayed on one side were the forces of order, clerical authority, education, tradition, and reverence for the past, who called themselves the "Old Lights."[7] The "New Lights," on the other hand, emphasized the individual authority of the inner spirit and the need for men's hearts to be quickened with the knowledge of the love of God. The conservatives were convinced that the New Light doctrines would produce intellectual and social chaos; and though their worst fears may have been exaggerated, the revival spirit did bring about fundamental change. Suddenly lay men and women were convinced that they could have self-authenticating religious experience which made them independent of professional clergy and church synods. Lay authority in the church became greater; and this same line of thinking, when applied to the political sphere, was an unquestionable boost to democratic theory. Ironically, the Great Awakening contributed to the Enlightenment spirit which swept young America in the course of the eighteenth century.[8]

The reaction to the Great Awakening is a classic example of the truth of the proposition that theological insights, if they capture the popular mind, can bring about significant change. Whether they intended it or not, the New Lights set in motion a movement which was perceived as a threat to the predominant American social and intellectual patterns because they successfully introduced a new notion of religious authority.

2

A LEADER PREPARED: THE ADVENT OF REVIVAL

Just as the Great Awakening did not appear in New England suddenly and without warning, so too Jonathan Edwards did not move to center stage without a great deal of preparation. Born in the parsonage in East Windsor, Connecticut, on October 5, 1703, Edwards was the fifth child and only son among his parents' eleven children. His family was comfortable and well-connected. Grandfather Solomon Stoddard was one of the most important and influential ministers of his time, and Edwards' paternal grandfather was a wealthy merchant in Hartford. Jonathan Edwards was prepared for college by his father, Timothy, a successful and learned, but not distinguished, minister. When he entered Yale College in 1716, it was a struggling, tiny institution still without a permanent home. Edwards, a deliberate and serious student, was graduated in 1720 and became minister of a Scotch Presbyterian church in New York City. He was tutor at Yale from 1724 to 1727, when he was ordained at Northampton, Massachusetts, as associate to his Grandfather Stoddard. Shortly after settling in Northampton, Edwards married Sarah Pierrepont, of the eminent Pierrepont family of New Haven. Stoddard died in 1729, leaving his twenty-six-year-old grandson as minister of the most prestigious church in Massachusetts outside of Boston.[9]

Northampton had not only been the seat of the "river god" who controlled the churches of the Connecticut River valley, it had also hosted Stoddard's famous "harvests." In 1733 and 1734 Northampton again was visited with revivals. The young Edwards preached in several communities along the river as word spread of the wondrous awakenings in Northampton. Edwards was not content, however, merely to "host" the awakenings; as a natural intellectual, he sought to understand and to explicate the curious events. *A Faithful Narrative of the Surprising Work of God*, published in 1737, was the revision of a letter to his friend, the Rev. Benjamin Colman of Boston. It sought, in a remarkably objective manner, to report on the events of the Northampton revival, placing primary stress on the unexpected nature of the occurrences. The minister gave himself no credit; he had not induced the revival; it was the result of God's activity; he merely hosted it and then witnessed startling behavioral change. While once it was difficult to get people to refrain from exclusive concern for worldly affairs, the revival turned their attention to matters of religion. Now Edwards worried that his people were tempted "to neglect worldly affairs too much, and to spend too much time in the immediate exercise of religion."[10]

The *Narrative* forced Edwards to go through the intellectually rigorous exercise of trying to account for the "surprising conversions." Unlike later revival experiences in American religion, these early manifestations were neither planned nor expected. Edwards regarded his job as that of a reporter of events he had witnessed. In no sense did the minister set out to "create" the revival spirit. His conclusions predisposed him to accept the Great Awakening, when it came several years later, as a gift from God.

The advent of the Great Awakening resulted in a bitter controversy between those who were congenial to the phenomenon and those who opposed it. The colonies were ablaze not only with pro-revival fervor but also with heated opposition from conservatives who feared the revivalists' lack of propriety and recognized their potential for disorder. When emotions were at fever pitch, Jonathan Edwards was invited by his alma mater to preach the Commencement sermon. He did not shy away from the controversy; indeed, he was intellectually prepared for it.

The sermon Edwards preached to the Connecticut establishment assembled at Yale in September 1741 was entitled "Distinguishing Marks of a Work of the Spirit of God applied to that uncommon operation that has lately appeared on the minds of many of the people of New England." In his typically careful way, Edwards began by pointing out that not all signs of the revival were necessarily the result of God's grace. "Tears, trembling, groans, loud outcries, agonies of body, or the failing of bodily strength," for instance, were not infallible indications of genuine piety.[11]

Turning from the negative signs, Edwards noted that positive signs also could be attributed to the revival. Increased interest in the things of the spirit, in the scriptures, in the church, and in devotions to Christian charity, he announced, "plainly shew *the finger of God*, and are sufficient to outweigh a thousand such little objections, as many make from oddities, irregularities, errors in conduct, and the delusions and scandals of some professors."[12] Not all the effects of the revivals were clearly God-given, but it was equally unwarranted to reject the possibility that the heightened affections were the result of God's Spirit. The Old Lights were especially angered at Edwards' conclusion "*that the extraordinary influence that had lately appeared, causing an uncommon concern and engagedness of mind about the things of religion, is undoubtedly, in the general, from the Spirit of God.*"[13] Edwards thus established himself as a leader of the pro-revivalist group and guaranteed that he would never again be invited to preach at Yale.

3

GOD'S SOVEREIGNTY AND THE "SENSE OF THE HEART"

Edwards was decidedly unlike Whitefield, the Tennents, Davenport, or any of the other itinerant evangelists because of his genius for philosophical analysis. His commitment to the revival grew out of a sophisticated and rigorously turned intellectual position. The Awakenings were not only the setting and context but also the impetus for Edwards' work. The revivals became a case study from which was to emerge an epistemology worthy of his genius. In 1742 he published *Some Thoughts Concerning the Present Revival of Religion in New England* (John Wesley had it reprinted in England), and in 1746 his great *Treatise Concerning the Religious Affections* was complete.

Edwards did not merely affirm revivalism; he sought to understand the reality of religious experience and to seek some means of identifying *authenticity* in experience. As in his Yale sermon, he never claimed that all emotional response was of God, but he refused to discount the possibility that the Holy Spirit moved in men in ways not easily comprehensible to human reason. Edwards proposed a positive theology in which the essence of true religion was affection.

"I am bold to assert," he wrote, "that there never was any considerable change wrought in the mind of any person, by anything of a religious nature that he read, heard or saw, who had not his affections moved."[14] Truth came to men not in a calculated rational way but through the "sense of the heart."

The knowledge of God, according to Edwards, involved more than rational consent; not that religion was irrational, but rather the category of "rationality" was itself insufficient. Faith was appropriated by the *whole man*, not merely by man the thinker: " 'Tis an evidence that true religion, or holiness of heart, lies very much in the affection of the heart, that the Scriptures place the sin of the heart very much in hardness of heart."[15]

The concept "heart" referred to the essential unification of the "mind" and "feeling" or "emotion" in Edwards' thought. Thus the "sense of the heart" was man's true knowledge, the knowledge that was beauty; not the mind alone but the mind coupled with the affections. To fail to be open to the affectional life was to miss the "sense of the heart"; it was to have "hardness of heart." Edwards preached the sermons for which he is popularly known because of his complex philosophical understanding of epistemology and psychology which grew out of his effort to investigate and conceptualize the experience of conversion he had known. No amount of study could result in faith; faith was affectional and immediate. "The informing of the understanding is all vain," he wrote, "any farther than it affects the heart: or which is the same thing, has influence on the affections."[16]

The affectional nature of true knowledge was tied to Edwards' overwhelming sense of God's sovereignty. Man could know nothing of God except as God revealed himself. The absolute sovereignty of God was thus the key principle of all he wrote. In his *Personal Narrative*, the account of his own conversion, Edwards told of first coming to the conviction of God's sovereignty: "I have often since had not only a conviction but a *delightful* conviction. The doctrine has very often appeared exceedingly pleasant, bright, and sweet. Absolute sovereignty is what I love to ascribe to God."[17] He further wrote: "My heart panted after this, to lie low before God, as in the dust; that I might be nothing, and that God might be ALL."[18]

The great treatises on *Freedom of the Will* and *Original Sin* were intended to explicate and to protect God's sovereignty. Edwards castigated Arminianism because he felt it emphasized man's role in the grand drama of life. One scholar has suggested that Edwards early sensed the future course of American religion. He opposed Arminianism not so much because he held to a behaviorist determinism but because he recoiled in horror from what would be the consequences for the American mind of an inflated doctrine of man.[19]

The dominant theme of Edwards' theology was God's self-sufficiency, infinite independence, and total omnipotence. This high doctrine of God's sovereignty was of immense consequence for religious authority, when coupled, as it was in Edwards, with the epistemological conviction that God revealed himself personally, immediately, experientially to individual men through the affections of the heart.

True knowledge of the sovereign God was dependent on the affections; thus, authority for religion was tied to the immediate vitalizing reality of God in the human heart. No complex of propositional beliefs, creedal affirmations, or traditional formulations guaranteed religious truth; "true religion," wrote Edwards, "consists so much in the affections that there can be *no true religion* without them."[20] The Northampton minister did not *reduce* religion to the affections—indeed, he made it clear that true religion was *more* than affection—but without the affections, faith did not exist.[21] The thrust of the argument was to undercut the stereotyped religious views predominant in the late seventeenth and early eighteenth centuries. God's truth was to be known personally and affectionally; the multiple norms of scripture, creedal affirmation, and church tradition were important, but each was ultimately dependent upon the reality of God to the human heart.

4

AUTHORITY FOR THEOLOGY: THE IMMEDIACY OF REVELATION

In the final analysis, Jonathan Edwards placed the seat of religious authority within the individual believer. Once a person's affections had been kindled and the truth of God was immediately known to him, any imposition of religious authority from outside was not only unnecessary but scandalous. The test of religious truth consisted in man's inward experience rather than outward assent to rational propositions. Christian faith was in no sense an exercise of intellectual agreement to creeds or orthodox convictions but a witness in the depth of one's whole being, and once achieved it was certain and authoritative.

Edwards wrote, of course, prior to the advent of the sophisticated theories of science and historical criticism which would later introduce far more complex problems into any consideration of authority for theology. Nevertheless, the implications for theology of his grounding of religious authority in the "sense of the heart" frontally challenged the theological writing of colonial New England, which, for the most part, repaired to the authorities of scripture and the Puritan tradition and largely distrusted reliance upon the individual conscience. Theological writing, usually in sermonic form, tended to be scholastic. Edwards proposed an alternative. He certainly used scripture and church tradition without hesitation, but methodologically the authority of the "sense of the heart" was primary. His theology, which was the basis for his preaching, was not intended to be apologetic. Theological authority was independent of man's judgment. The theologian's job was to examine and present the faith in a clear, systematic statement; it was not to justify the faith to man.

The theological position Edwards articulated was thoroughly revelational; God's authoritative revelation was antecedent to man's knowledge of God. God revealed himself according to his will, and man's appropriation of revelation was through the "sense of the heart." God could be known only through his grace given according to his pleasure, but Edwards' epistemological position made God's relationship to man immediate, by grounding man's knowledge of God in the holy affections. Authority for theology, then, was based not on external propositions but on internal awareness of God's glory. Priority was given to experiential rather than speculative divinity. This meant that the "sense of the heart" became both content and norm for theology.

An example of Edwards' methodology for theological construction illustrates the functional significance of the authority of revelation. One of Edwards' central theological affirmations was his conviction that God ordained and ordered all creation according to his pleasure. Throughout history, men have pondered the question as to the meaning of the multiple factors which combine to equal man's experience of existence. Strong conviction of transcendent being qualifies the question to the extent that any answer must be given in terms of divine order. According to Edwards, the world was not created either for its inherent beauties or for man's good; these ends are superficial and ultimately irrelevant. The order of creation had at base a specific and singular purpose: the glorification of God. This thesis he set out to explain in his *Dissertation on the End for which God Created the World.*[22]

In the *Dissertation*, Edwards argued with logical precision, examining carefully the dictates of reason and the teachings of the scrip-

tures. He appealed to the tradition of the church as faithful interpreters have tried to understand God's intention in creation. The crux
of authority, however, was dealt with at the outset and was affirmed
rather than argued. Certain givens were announced which were revealed knowledge accessible to man because of God's grace. The
suitability of theological understandings was determined with regard
to revealed insights. These revealed insights, in the final analysis, were
known by the individual through immediate relationship with God.
Thus, at the beginning of the *Dissertation*, Edwards wrote, "Indeed,
this affair seems properly to be an affair of divine revelation. In order
to be determined what was designed in the creating of the astonishing
fabric of the universe we behold, it becomes us to attend to, and rely
on, what *HE* has told us, who was the architect."[23] Complex elements of the nature of the created order were revealed through
scripture, church teachings, and observation of the natural world; but
the essential affirmation that the created order was to serve and
glorify God was revealed personal knowledge which became authoritative, since, in matters theological, Christians were to be "*principally*
guided by divine revelation."[24]

Edwards examined reason and determined that the dictates of
reason, rightly understood, made plain that God's end in his creation
"is not unreasonable."[25] Though God's truth was not unreasonable,
reason was, in itself, insufficient; only revelation truly allowed men
knowledge of God. Turning to the scriptures, Edwards examined
numerous passages which he found to point in the same direction as
did the insights of reason:

> The great end of God's works, which is so variously expressed in
> scripture, is indeed but ONE; and this *one* end is most properly
> and comprehensively called, *THE GLORY OF GOD*; by which
> name it is most commonly called in scripture; and is fitly com-
> pared to an effulgence or emanation of light from a luminary.[26]

Scripture for Edwards was the primary vehicle of God's revelation;
it was, as such, authoritative. He was always careful to insist that
immediate revelation did not *supplant* scripture.[27] The Bible was
understood to be *consistent* with revelation. Here, of course, was an
example of Edwards' precritical stance. None of the problematic
issues of biblical authorship or interpretation, which were later to
emerge, occupied his attention. The Bible functioned normatively as a
guide; it was a witness to revelation against which the affections were
to be *tested*. But, in fact, Edwards did distinguish among biblical

mandates. Divergent interpretations were legion even before sophisticated criticism. The Bible needed interpretation; Edwards' use of the Bible presupposed a prior revelation by which man was able to understand the multiple elements of God's biblical revelation.[28] The prior revelation was God himself, as sovereign Lord of all creation, in communion with the heart of man.

Edwards' theological genius consisted in breaking away from scholastic proposition, fidelity to church tradition, or treatment of prior theological writings. He sought a recovery of theology by opening it to the authority of God's vital immediate presence to the individual of faith, thus freeing the theological task from exclusive dependence on earthly mediate authority. Theology was freed from convention and stereotype, and freed for a new affirmation of God's sovereign independence and infinite grace. The initiator of, and authority for, theological reflection was the vitalizing relationship between the heart and mind of faith and the God of all creation.

5

AUTHORITY AND ETHICAL REFLECTION

The practical ethical implications of Edwards' view of religious authority understandably upset the conservative clergy of New England. The strong conviction of God's sovereignty, coupled with the lodging of religious authority within the experience of individual revelation, permitted the possibility of a serious challenge to the usual complacency of the established order. As one scholar suggests, "The preaching of Jonathan Edwards contained within itself the seeds of revolution, both for the eighteenth century and for the twentieth."[29] Edwards took little cognizance of the social and political issues which agitated the colonies.[30] Apparently he did not see the relationship between his radical religious revision and the potential for similar opposition to the assumptions of the inherited group norms.

Edwards laid bare one of the fundamental problems in Christian ethics: How is God's authority mediated in the world? Most Christians will agree that God is ultimately authoritative; disagreement arises with the attempt to describe the way in which God's will and intentions are translated in such a way that they become operative for individual and corporate life. In fact, by choosing to make man's inner light, infused with God's quickening spirit, uniquely authoritative, Edwards shunned the difficult problem of the social order and moved directly to the infinitely grander scale of transcendent divinity. The primary ethical arena for Edwards was to be the heavenly vision rather than penultimate order.

Edwards' theological conviction that the reason for, and meaning of, all creation was God's glory, as set forth in the *Dissertation on the End for which God Created the World*, rendered meaningless any distinction between secular and church history. He believed it possible to trace God's actions on man's behalf in the events and issues of the world. Edwards always intended to write a "History of the Work of Redemption" in which he would interpret God's actions in relation to man's finite designs. He never finished this most ambitious of all his projects, but sermons and outlines on the subject were published in 1774.[31]

From creation through the incarnation, and from the resurrection to the end of time, Edwards interpreted the whole history of the world from the perspective of the scriptural account of God's redemption of his chosen people. The central theme was that the various peoples and events of the world were steadily and inevitably moving toward the grand conclusion which was to be the light of the pure glory of God. The interpretation of the work of redemption is perhaps the best example of the way in which Edwards' thinking radically relativized temporal matters. Nothing was absolute or ultimately important except God, whose sovereign will ordered the totality of being according to his own glory.

The beatific vision dealt with historically in Work of Redemption was set forth supremely in the posthumous essay *The Nature of True Virtue*. Perhaps no piece of Edwards' writing is more variously provocative. Characteristically, Edwards produced a lofty definition when he sought to explore the meaning of virtue: "True virtue most essentially consists in BENEVOLENCE TO BEING IN GENERAL. Or perhaps, to speak more accurately, it is that consent, propensity and union of heart to being in general, which is immediately exercised in a good will."[32] The consequence of the definition was that true virtue meant pure *love to God*, because God, the supreme unity of all virtue and excellence, was the most excellent and most all-encompassing being, or "being in general."

> God is not only infinitely greater and more excellent than all other being, but he is the head of the universal system of existence; the foundation and fountain of all being and all beauty; from whom all is perfectly dependent; of whom, and through whom, and to whom is all being and all perfection; and whose

being and beauty are, as it were, the sum and comprehension of all existence and excellence; much more than the sun is the fountain and summary comprehension of all the light and brightness of the day.[33]

The implications of equating all being with God are potentially unorthodox. It is possible to argue that the logical conclusion of Edwards' position is pantheism. Edwards was caught on the horns of a dilemma because he recognized the problems of both theism, which emphasizes the separation between God and his creation, and pantheism, which unites them. One interpreter claims that Edwards' corpus is an effort to achieve a "third way" and define a synthesis of "majesty and immediacy."[34] One provocative argument states that "in substance, the God of Jonathan Edwards was a supremely excellent Christian commonwealth."[35] This statement is open to misinterpretation. Edwards never lost his Calvinistic sense of God's incontrovertible otherness. Nevertheless, the truth of the claim lies in the fact that Edwards' ultimate vision was indeed one of perfect unity in which *all* individual distinction would be obliterated. Such perfection, of course, was not to be achieved on earth. Though unattainable in human community, true beauty and virtue became Edwards' guiding standard according to which he judged all else as inferior.

Edwards thus insisted that the *appearance* of virtue in *men's* eyes was not a true test. Only love to being in general—God—was true virtue; and such love was not available to man except by God's grace, which was given strictly according to God's pleasure.[36] Man, by himself, could achieve no moral good.

Private affection, partial concern, and utilitarian interest paled in comparison to true virtue. It was not that they were of no value, but that they were inferior because they were limited to finite existence. One scholar suggests that *The Nature of True Virtue* was intended to undercut mere concern for social policy and redirect moral thought to the plane of high expectations: "The point of this extreme idealization of the concept of virtue in Edwards' thought is to offset the tendencies of an attitude in morals which had already become prominent in his day, and which now is almost universal—the reduction of philosophical ethics to applied sociology."[37] According to Edwards, there existed an unbridgeable gap between true virtue and operative functional virtue for men in community; the latter was clearly inferior.

The key to Edwards' ethical analysis was his theological conviction that the universe was ordered solely for God's own glory. God's order became the ideal norm for human endeavor, and all else was second-ary. Edwards knocked the props out from under the old Puritan system, which understood God's authority to manifest itself in a hierarchical pattern for the governance of man's social life. All hope of man's knowing or doing anything really good in this earthly sphere was stripped away to reveal the incomprehensible Divinity, the wholeness and perfectness of God's beauty, which alone was good. Edwards' religious insight was supremely dysfunctional in terms of the practical problems of the social order.[38]

The Northampton minister's conviction about church policy must be understood in light of the vision which inspired *The Nature of True Virtue*. For many years Edwards was content to follow in the shoes of his revered Grandfather Stoddard in regard to church membership and open communion, but gradually he became convinced that the earlier Puritan intention—a community of regenerate visible saints—was the true and proper course for the church.

By closing communion and seeking to realize a genuine community of visible saints, Edwards was seeking to create proleptically a vision of the ultimate community in which all would be one in God. Edwards tried to impose his decision on the Northampton church, but a congregation long accustomed to the ways of the eminent grandfather was unwilling to indulge the grandson in what appeared to be his whim. One interpreter has argued that when Edwards was dismissed from his pulpit in 1750, he was "a victim of the widespread unrest between clergy and laity over the matter of authority."[39] Edwards was unable to have his way; his people did not fathom the depth of his conviction or the height of his vision.

Relatively early in his career, Edwards wrote: "All who are truly religious are not of this world."[40] The ethical analysis contained in *The Nature of True Virtue* illustrates why the truly religious are not of this world. For the religious man, as Edwards understood him, all earthly matters are relativized over against the singular vision of the blinding Divinity. Affairs of the world ultimately pass; only God endures.

One cannot turn to Edwards for a system of theological ethics; there is none to be found. Jonathan Edwards' brilliant insights were not primarily concerned with human action. His work sought to achieve an unencumbered sense of the true virtue of the glory of God. Unlike his forefathers, who very much concerned themselves with this world as well as the next, Edwards shattered the worldly; yet the impetus for his work was the social setting in which he found himself. Men were alienated from religion because of the use to which ministers and civil magistrates had put it. Men needed to be reminded once again of the possibility of being in immediate relationship to God. Edwards chose to explore the difficult problems facing religious quest and belief in a time of fervent awakening and gradual rational Enlightenment. He recognized that the central problem facing theologian, clergyman, and layman was the issue of authority. His achievement was a theology which emphasized the overwhelming experiential reality of God to individual man.

By placing absolute authority in the revelation of God to the soul, Edwards challenged the system of hierarchical authority which had been espoused by the original settlers. He sought to recover a sense of God's absolute sovereignty, but he rejected the earlier scheme by which God's authority was translated into the world for the sake of social order. Edwards concerned himself with the grand order of the universe, the ultimate end of all creation.

Because human beings have always had to live with penultimate problems, and because few are capable of sustaining an Edwardean beatific vision, true as it may be, some Christians have always worried about making the reality of God meaningful for human society. Edwards regarded such effort as secondary and finally impossible, because of the absolutely relativizing nature of the highest truth and virtue. He may be charged with impracticability, but such a challenge pales before Edwards' positive charge that the religious problem is with those who insist that faith must be practical.

CHAPTER II

AUTHORITY AND COMMON LIFE: HORACE BUSHNELL

1

THEOLOGICAL CONTROVERSY AND THE AUTHORITY OF THE AUTONOMOUS INDIVIDUAL

Not until 1847, almost one hundred years after Jonathan Edwards' death, did Horace Bushnell's first important publication, *Discourses on Christian Nurture*, come off the presses. The intervening years witnessed multiple divisions within the Calvinist family as efforts to respond to changing cultural realities produced conflicting claims with regard to authority for religious doctrines and teachings. Bushnell's theology can be understood best within the context of continuing controversy.

Edwards had been followed by disciples trained in his own Northampton parsonage; of these, Samuel Hopkins and Joseph Bellamy were the most important. Though they sought to remain faithful to Edwardean teaching, they nevertheless introduced slight variations of consequence. Hopkins sapped the vitality of his mentor's theology by systematizing it into a rigorous construct set forth in his two-volume *System of Doctrines*.[1] Although Hopkins carefully maintained the Edwardean notion that church membership should be restricted to those who had clear personal conviction of God's regenerating grace, he compromised his teacher's position in regard to original sin and thus opened the door for subtle but significant deviation from Edwards' anthropology.[2] This qualification, which allowed a greater freedom for human will, was sufficient to begin the gradual erosion of strict Calvinism which came with the effort to take cognizance of the republican Enlightenment.

Joseph Bellamy was exercised by the curious paradox between the Calvinist affirmation of an all-powerful God dealing with men according to his own pleasure and the New Light emphasis on the importance of repentance and acceptance of God's grace on man's part. He argued that God permitted sin in order to illustrate man's need of him and his gracious love. Christian redemption, through the act of Jesus Christ, brought about an increment in God's glory and man's potential happiness. Man needed to repent in order to be forgiven, though there was no guarantee that every one who repented would be saved. Bellamy thus attempted at once to protect God's sovereignty and the rightful place of revival.[3]

Although Hopkins and Bellamy left the door slightly ajar to the humanistic concerns of the late eighteenth century, they appear rigid in comparison to the Old Light Calvinists, many of whom had thoroughly imbibed the spirit of the Enlightenment. The former distinctions were soon to crumble, however, as New England witnessed a new ordering of theological parties. In an attempt to undercut the significant inroads made by Enlightenment and Deistic sentiment in the course of the eighteenth century, a moderate group of Calvinists, led by Jonathan Edwards' remarkable grandson, President Timothy Dwight of Yale, broke from the conservative Edwardeans just before the turn of the century and sought to inject new life into traditional orthodoxy by offering a fresh interpretation. Going further than either Hopkins or Bellamy in regard to the freedom of man's will, Dwight became a staunch advocate of revivalism and determined to sweep New England in opposition to growing liberalism.

Unitarianism, the most notable manifestation of the liberal movement, complained of the scholasticism of orthodoxy and flatly rejected the Trinity; it discounted Calvinism's low estimate of man's nature and put aside the doctrine of original sin; it insisted that if God were really good he would not predestine any man to ultimate damnation. Unitarians did not recognize as authoritative either the Bible or church tradition.[4] The rejection of any authority external to man's reason or conscience encouraged schism, and in 1836 a group which became known as Transcendentalists determined that the Unitarian revolt had not gone far enough.[5]

The Unitarian and Transcendentalist movements were regarded with profound horror by traditional Calvinists, who founded Andover Seminary in 1808 to combat the errors in divinity being perpetrated by Harvard, the Unitarian bastion. Andover and a new seminary in Hartford were supported by Old Calvinists and Edwardeans, former enemies who now, in the face of liberal apostasy, combined forces under the leadership of Leonard Woods and Bennet Tyler. This conservative group, which came to be known as the Tylerites, did not encompass all of orthodoxy, however. A group of moderates, the spiritual descendants of Timothy Dwight, controlled Yale Divinity School and looked to Nathaniel W. Taylor for leadership.

Yale was the corporate advocate of "New Haven Theology," and Taylor was its chief expositor. The distinctions were fine, but the chief modification offered by Taylor to Edwards' work had to do with man's free will and the extent to which he could be held morally accountable given the doctrine of God's absolute sovereignty. New Haven theologians set for themselves the task of demonstrating that the strict Calvinist notion of God did not rule out man's moral agency.[6] To conservative spokesman Bennet Tyler, this appeared to be not mere modification but wholesale reconstruction.

To give Taylor his due, he was struggling not simply to maintain the continuity of the Edwardean faith but to adapt old truths to new realities. The Enlightenment had penetrated so deeply into American intellectual life that its effects were being seen in popular thinking as well as in the assumptions of sophisticated scholars. Post-Revolutionary Americans tended to be optimistic about man's abilities to make accurate judgments based on reason—even with regard to religious teachings and the sufficiency of the Bible.

The subtle adjustments of religious doctrine which have been documented reflect an effort to seek some modest accommodation between prevailing cultural norms and traditional Christian convictions. Whenever conditions require that the primary theological task be interpretation, the question of authority arises. Authority for religious warrant was at base the issue in both the Unitarian rejection of orthodoxy and the Transcendentalist revolt against Unitarianism. The multiple divisions within Calvinism, largely begun as a result of the Great Awakening, were exacerbated and perpetuated as a consequence of conflicting claims over authorization for particular formulations of doctrine and teaching.

Evidence has already been offered, with reference to Jonathan Edwards, that periods in which religious authority becomes especially problematic tend to coincide with times of social disintegration. This is not necessarily to argue a cause-and-effect sequence from either direction, but only to notice a relationship between seasons of social disorder and a lack of clarity and conviction in theology about the nature of its task and the validity of its claims.

Just as the individualism of the eighteenth-century Great Awakening sowed seeds of schism in the churches and disorder in the structures of society, so the individualistic spirit of the common man

22

had the same effect in the nineteenth century. Ironically, this rugged individualism was encouraged by the liberalism of Deism and Unitarianism, which elevated human reason and offered *intellectual* support for a high anthropology, *and* by the enthusiasm of the new revivals, which emphasized the Arminian doctrine of man's ability to choose his own salvation and thus provided *emotional* undergirding for a lofty doctrine of man. Though the liberalism of the intellectuals and the pietism of the revivalists approached man from radically different angles and significantly different styles, they both encouraged confidence in an increasingly autonomous individual and thus offered no strong opposition to the generalized social disorder which prevailed in nineteenth-century America.

In contrast to the early American sense of society as an ordered whole consisting of multiple dependent variables, each of which was necessary to the well-being of the rest, the early nineteenth century was characterized by unplanned growth and affirmation of fierce independence. Celebration of the common man did not encourage appeal to authority outside of the individual; it was assumed that the good of the community was best served by individual enterprise. Popular religious teachings made few claims to provide guidance for corporate life, and neither liberal nor revivalist Christianity was able to separate authority convincingly from the feelings or inclinations of disparate believers. The stage was thus clearly set for the appearance of a new orientation to the problem of authority.

2

TOWARD A MINISTRY OF THEOLOGICAL REFORMULATION

Horace Bushnell was born in the township of Litchfield, Connecticut, on April 14, 1802, and was raised on a small farm amidst the gentle hills of southern New England.[7] Bushnell's father, not among the economic or intellectual elite, supplemented his agricultural income by running a cloth-finishing mill and a wool-carding factory. Bushnell frequently recalled that he wore "homespun" in college. The family was closely knit, laboring, reading, playing, and worshiping together. Simple and unpretentious people, the Bushnells displayed supportive interest in the activities of the four boys and two girls; the parents placed special emphasis upon personal discipline and education.

Bushnell's early religious training was far from perfunctory. Both his mother, who had been raised an Episcopalian, and his father, formerly a Methodist, were active in the life of the Congregational

Church and, true to their own religious antecedents, did not wait for conversion in their children but always treated them as Christians growing in the faith. Horace Bushnell was hesitant to enter college even though his parents urged him to do so; cognizant of his modest social standing, he was certain he would be out of place. When he finally entered Yale College in September of 1823, it was because he had joined the church and had notions of entering the ministry.

An able student, Bushnell was graduated with the A.B. degree in 1827; meanwhile, however, second thoughts about the ministry induced him to accept a teaching job in Norwich. He disliked teaching school and after a trial of only a few months joined the staff of the *Journal of Commerce*, a recently established New York daily newspaper. While serving as associate editor, Bushnell decided to return to Yale and study law. A year later, President Jeremiah Day offered him a position as tutor in the college, a job which he performed with great success. Tutors generally stayed only a year or two—a kind of postgraduate fellowship for advanced study—and then moved on, usually to the ministry or to law. Bushnell passed the bar examination and planned to enter private practice, but, during 1831, a religious revival swept Yale which left deep impressions and caused him once again to consider the ministry. His theological education at Yale Divinity School began in 1831.

Nathaniel W. Taylor was at the height of his powers during Bushnell's years in the Divinity School. No student escaped thorough exposure to Taylor's system, but Bushnell was never satisfied with his brilliant teacher's theology. Taylor seemed hopelessly rigid and scholastic. Bushnell was older than most of his Divinity School colleagues, and his experience and maturity no doubt contributed to his independence. A crucial factor in his hesitance to accept Taylor's doctrine was his previous acquaintance with the writing of Samuel Taylor Coleridge, whose *Aids to Reflection* had been published in the United States in 1829. Bushnell had read this book as an undergraduate and returned to it again during his year as a tutor. Late in life he admitted that he was more indebted to this book than any other single volume except the Bible.[8] Perhaps the most important aspect of Coleridge's work was its frontal assault on the logical foundations assumed to be necessary for philosophical and theological formulation. Coleridge stressed the intuitional and affectional nature of knowledge and provided an alternative to the epistemological theory which assumed that truth could and must be captured in creed and dogma.

Having found the New Haven theology uncongenial, Bushnell had no ready-made theology when he accepted the pastorate of North Church, Hartford, in 1833. What he did have was the wisdom to see that careful theological reformulation was necessary if Christianity were to be released from the shackles to which scholasticism had confined it.[9]

3

THE ORGANISMIC PRINCIPLE AND PERSONAL KNOWLEDGE OF GOD

Horace Bushnell became convinced that the theology of the Great Awakening and its subsequent interpretations had greatly exaggerated the role of the individual to the detriment of Christianity. In reflecting on mid-eighteenth-century revivalism, Bushnell admitted that it played the positive role of displacing "an era of dead formality," but its serious defect was that it made "nothing of the family, and the church, and the organic powers God has constituted as vehicles of Grace."[10] Bushnell sought to provide an alternative to individualism because of his strong theological conviction that human life was fundamentally social. It would have been easier to accommodate himself to the prevailing norms; the individualistic theology of revivalism was congenial to the dominant values of the prevailing culture. Writing in a time when the glories of the unique common man and his untutored mind were being celebrated not only politically but philosophically in America, Bushnell argued that basic humanity depended on relationships with a variety of groups. Any claim to individuality needed qualification: "We possess only a mixed individuality all our life long. A pure, separate, individual man, living *wholly* within and from himself, is a mere fiction."[11]

Discourses on Christian Nurture, in which Bushnell applied his organic theory to the traditional teaching of New England Congregationalism regarding conversion, met with such controversy that the Massachusetts Sabbath School Society, its publisher, soon withdrew the little volume. Though the debate about conversion was not new to New England theology, orthodox thinkers considered the matter settled. The Half-Way Covenant and Solomon Stoddard's lowering of the bar to Holy Communion had been, in part at least, intended to extend the ministry of the church to persons who had not experienced a satisfactory conversion. Jonathan Edwards, when he decided that such revision was unjustified, greatly tightened church order in an effort, insofar as humanly possible, to make the church a pure community of saints. His successors applied his doctrine with rigor.

Bushnell was unhappy with any theory that tied church membership to conversion. He was unwilling to restrict the work of the Holy Spirit to seasons of quickening; furthermore, the assumption that the conversion experience could be adequately described by the candidate and accurately judged by church members as genuine seemed to need fresh examination. Arguing that life was organic, with all individual experiences interrelated and mutually qualified, Bushnell recommended that children be trained up from birth to think of themselves as growing into the Christian faith. Conversion might take numerous forms, Bushnell suggested, and the Christian community was derelict in its duty if it failed to provide for the creation of an environment of nurture which would offer locus and occasion for the individual to come into immediate relationship with God. The concept of Christian nurture, however, was designed to do far more than reassess the place of conversion in the church and redirect the style of the church's ministry to children.

The major thrust of Bushnell's first publication was to undercut the exclusive attention to individual faith which tended to dominate the church in his time. The issue was authority: How was individual experience to be confirmed or tested? How would the church order its life if it had to contend with a multiplicity of immediate revelations? On the other hand, how could the church relinquish the principle of immediate revelation and avoid dogmatic authoritarianism? Christian nurture was the theoretical underpinning for the affirmation that religious authority had its seat neither in the immediate individual experience nor in tradition and community, but in a complex interaction of the two. Only if individuality could be tempered, though not destroyed, would it be possible for the Christian faith to exert normative influence on matters of everyday social life.

The beatific vision of Edwards made it difficult if not impossible to translate religion meaningfully for the practical ordering of life. Bushnell argued that, for Edwards, religion was "a kind of transcendental matter, which belongs on the outside of life, and has no part in the laws by which life is organized"; this meant that religion had no "vital connection with the ties, and causes, and forms, and habits, which constitute the frame of our history."[12] Such a position was anathema to the Hartford minister.

In Bushnell's time, the proliferation of theological parties, and the contentions within and among them, was the harvest of the seeds sown by the Edwardean emphasis on the exclusive authority of the

26

individual relationship with the sovereign God. Edwards had worked in social circumstances significantly different from those of Bushnell. The Northampton of Edwards' day was rural and pastoral; community was "built-in"; it did not occur to persons in the frontier of the Connecticut River valley to deny the reality of organic interdependence. Edwards had to fight to make people see that the community of visible saints, with its doctrinal Calvinism inherited from the exiled fathers, needed supplementation with the transcendent immediacy of God to the individual. Bushnell, however, lived in an urban setting which was beginning to industrialize, a setting which had lost the characteristic feeling of organic unity of previous decades. This decay of community was exacerbated by religious individualism, which, Bushnell insisted, had "burst the bonds of church authority, and erected the individual mind into a tribunal of judgment within itself."[13] Bushnell's problem was to assert the principle of the organic unity of men without losing the reality of God in the heart of the individual Christian.

The issue of authority which lay behind the debates energizing the theological community toward the middle of the nineteenth century had two aspects. The first was epistemological and had to do with what could be taught and believed theologically. The second was practical and concerned the way in which Christian teachings might aid in ordering common life. Bushnell endeavored to remind Christians that God had provided institutions for the ordering of life which, in matters of both faith and practice, were "to some extent, at least, sovereign over the individual man."[14] Examination of the New Testament scriptures would demonstrate, he argued, that God had ordained three primary institutions for the ordering of human life: the state, the church, and the family. Individualism undermined these "three great forms of organic existence."[15]

Bushnell's concern was not to establish a hierarchy of external institutional authority which would legislate and regularize human life; far from it, he always insisted that a wide range of personal options for the individual must not only be tolerated but encouraged.[16] In both church and society he fought regimentation.[17] There is a difference, though, between the kind of pluralism Bushnell envisioned and the anarchy of radical individualism. Neither rigid conformity nor mindless independence was to be valued.

The family, the church, and the state, as organic institutions ordained by God, functioned to guide and to test the individual of faith.[18] This did not mean, however, that Bushnell placed authority exclusively in community. The community, even the community of saints, could become authoritarian or dogmatic. Christian faith could not be divorced from the community, and common life functions as both base and authority for the Christian, but priority was given to the conception of faith as a uniquely personal matter of the heart.

In a thoughtful sermon entitled "The Immediate Knowledge of God," Bushnell explicated the "distinction between knowing God, and knowing about God."[19] The distinction was between having theoretical knowledge of church history, theology, Bible, and doctrine, and having "immediate, personal" knowledge of God himself.[20] Referring to the heated arguments about creed and doctrine so familiar to New England Congregationalists, Bushnell reminded his congregation that no human formulation of Christianity could possibly do justice to the unfathomable truths of faith because, no matter how learned, they could only be partial and relative. Furthermore, no amount of disciplined study could induce faith; for this reason, Bushnell urged his contemporaries to take doctrinal arguments less seriously. "No man," he told the Harvard Divinity School, "is in the Christian state till he gets by, and, in one sense, beyond reflective action."[21]

The intent was not to reject rigorous theological thinking; Bushnell only wished modesty to inform scholarly reflection. Study was important and contributive to individual growth in the faith; the use of what he called "medial knowledges," including books and other teachings, provided occasion for growth and guidance in things spiritual.[22] His protest was against the kind of doctrinal narrowness which had rent New England Congregationalism asunder. Tense theological argumentation caused dissension and division in the church and diverted attention from the primary task of the Christian: namely, growth in the personal knowledge of God. In a lecture delivered at Andover Seminary, Bushnell, having asserted his position, drove relentlessly to his conclusion that it would be better "to practice any severity, rather than to attempt the knowledge of God by the mere natural understanding."[23]

Bushnell's insistence on the need for immediate knowledge of God, as opposed to familiarity with theological systematics or church doctrine, raises a crucial question with regard to religious authority. Is the seat of authority the point of individual relationship with God? If so, does not that claim vitiate the prior claim that authority is inextricably bound to common life?

Interpreters have been inclined to emphasize Bushnell's rejection of external authority and have described him as the father of the liberal movement in American theology. This analysis has highlighted

Bushnell's relationship to Coleridge, Continental philosophy, and American romanticism. A recent study, for instance, states, "If he never read a page of German philosophy, he still revealed its influence, and in his insistence on the authority of the individual conscience he avowed the central precept of 'Self Reliance.' "[24] The problem with such an interpretation is that it understands Bushnell's stress on the individual conscience but misunderstands its meaning and consequences.

The contrast drawn between dogma and spirit and the insistence on the priority of spirit meant that no external authorizing agent could define or prescribe the necessary or correct lineaments of personal faith. Thus Bushnell said that "there is more of the true light of Christ in one hour of highest communion with him, than the best scheme of theological opinions has ever been able to offer."[25] Because ultimate religious reality was personal knowledge, religious authority did inhere in the individual conscience; but Bushnell's genius was such that he understood authority as more, but not less, than individual conscience precisely because of his conviction that one arrived at personal knowledge in a *context* of revelation which is common life. Bushnell suggested that preparation and nurture in Christianity were antecedent to the indispensable personal knowledge of God. "Christianity," he wrote, "is called 'spirit,' partly because it can truly enter and be apprehended by us, only as we are in it and of it, and have its spirit in us."[26]

Religious authority, according to Bushnell, inhered in common life not in the sense that the community established dictates of belief and practice but rather in that the juxtaposition of the Christian community and the personal interaction with God constituted the key to the discovery of true life. Faith, for Bushnell, as for Edwards, was the "sense of the heart"; but for Bushnell, it was always in *relationship to community*, even when it contradicted or offered direct prophetic challenge to the community. The Christian was thus *made* by common life and perpetually *remade* by the immediate transcendent reality of God. The organic communities of family, church, and nation provided continuity and authority, but they might become as dead as dogma; the revitalizing principle of the sense of the heart provided discontinuity and direct participation in the presence of the Divine. These two aspects of authority Bushnell always held together. The immediate sense of the heart was to be tested and confirmed in community; the community was tested, activated, and enriched by the transcendent reality of individual personal knowledge.

The complexity of Bushnell's concept of authority makes his

contribution of enduring importance. He knew that a final, singular answer was impossible, but he also knew that the issue was real and indispensable to theology. The implications of this theoretical combination of the sense of the heart and the authority of common life were great when applied to the task of the theologian.

4

AUTHORITY FOR THEOLOGY: THE MULTIPLE NORMS OF THE THEOLOGICAL TASK

Bushnell's disenchantment with logical, rigid scholasticism caused him to attempt a redirection of theology. He insisted that the task of theology was not to erect complete systems which could be judged true or false or could be used as standards by which individuals might be judged. Instead, he contended that theology was an exercise in service to ministry. Every minister ought to engage in theology in order to clarify and evaluate the meaning of the gospel for his particular setting; furthermore, the process of theology was more important than the final product. Unless the process were carefully undertaken, preaching was in danger of being disordered and unintelligible. Bushnell never spoke of a finished theological system but of the effort *toward* system; theology was a lifelong, ongoing process which would subject every assumption, every analysis, and every conclusion to perpetual examination.[27] The "endeavor after system" was considered to be of "greater benefit than the actually resulting systems prepared."[28]

The modest claims Bushnell made for theology were intended not to minimize its importance but to provide perspective. He early developed a theory of language which distinguished between the descriptive language dealing with material realities of an exact nature or property and the symbolic language of nonquantifiable values, theories, or art. The theory hinged on his conviction that there existed quantifiable, and thus absolute, ideas as well as nonmeasurable relative ideas: "In algebra and geometry, the ideas themselves being absolute, the terms or names also may be; but in mental science and religion, no such exactness is possible, because our apprehensions of truth are here only proximate and relative."[29]

Bushnell never deviated from his conviction that, in matters of spirit and religion, language could never be a sufficient vehicle for the expression of complete truth. Symbol and myth, which pointed beyond the language in which they were expressed, alone might approximate transcendent reality. "Poets, then, are the true meta-physicians, and if there be any complete science of man to come, they must bring it."[30] Theological formulation, thus hampered by language, was necessarily limited: "The principal difficulty we have with language now is, that it will not put into the theoretic under-standing what the imagination only can receive, and will not open to the head what the heart only can interpret."[31]

The conviction that language was incapable of adequately contain-ing theological truth serves to explain Bushnell's unwillingness to develop a systematic theology. It also suggests why he was never hesitant to become embroiled in heated theological controversy, to criticize established systems, and to advocate proliferation of fresh theological efforts. Every theological system was to be "open" for modification so that "incrustations" were not allowed to stifle new thinking.[32] Furthermore, the assumption that no logical system could ever be adequate suggested to Bushnell that the raw data of the theological task were not to be found merely in previous systematic efforts but in the *religious life*, and thus theology needed to be done within the context of the church.

The work of the theologian, then, is to seek to interpret, in a meaningful, creative, and contemporary manner, the reality of God and the nature of the gospel of Jesus Christ for men in the world. Because of the inadequacies of language there are inherent limitations to the theological enterprise, but the effort toward system helps to clarify and articulate difficult concepts and ancient truths. The theologian must endeavor to cultivate for himself the immediate knowledge of God, which experience is qualified and confirmed in light of the community of faith and articulated as contributive to the ongoing life of the community.

Given this description of the theological task, the question yet remains as to the methodological authority for constructive theology. Although all efforts are limited and relative, what are the criteria for making theological judgments and claims?

Bushnell's writing does not reflect the impact of either the Darwinian revolution or the development of historical criticism, both of which challenged old notions of religious authority and signifi-cantly shifted the nature of the discussion in the last quarter of the nineteenth century. Nevertheless, he did take account of the con-certed attacks on traditional affirmations generated by the Unitarian and Transcendentalist movements, both of which placed man's reason in ascendancy. Theodore Parker proclaimed, "I have sought my authority in the Nature of Man—in facts of consciousness within me, and facts of observation in the human world without."[33] Reflecting on his rupture with Unitarianism, Parker recalled, "I knew that I had thoroughly broken with the ecclesiastical authority of Christendom; its God was not my God, nor its Scriptures my Word of God, nor its Christ my Savior."[34]

Bushnell understood and sympathized with liberal affirmations of the reality of man's immediate experience of God, but he always insisted that immediate revelation be related to the life of the community. Source material for study in divinity, according to Bushnell, was to be found "in the Scripture, in the form of political and religious annals, the biographies of distinguished saints, the teachings of prophets, the incarnate life and death of the Word made flesh. Here opens a vast realm of divine fact, radiant in every part with the light of God."[35] Examination of Bushnell's procedural methodology reveals that he made use of each of the traditional sources of theological authority: scripture, creed, tradition, and experience.

Bushnell never felt the need to offer apologetics for his use of the Bible. His theological work was done within the context of the church and assumed openness on the part of the reader. Bushnell did not pride himself in the belief that anyone would become a Christian by reading his theology; his effort was toward clarification for the faithful. In *God in Christ* the dogmatic starting point was asserted: "I am speaking, mostly, to such as have faith to believe that the worlds were made, and find no difficulty in believing in God as a Creator."[36] The same assumption was made in regard to the Bible: "I am speaking, also, to such as believe the scriptures."[37] The decision to accept the Bible as a norm, however, does not eliminate the problem of authority; one must yet decide *how* the scriptures will function.

A literal interpretation of the Bible made no sense to Bushnell because of his theory of language, which denied that words could convey infinite truth. A slavish fidelity to word and phrase, or a dogmatic affirmation of biblical infallibility, he rejected in favor of a view which claimed that unique insight into ultimate truth was contained in the affective language of the holy scriptures. Precisely because biblical language was symbolic and poetic, it was intended to appeal not simply to man's reasoning faculty but to his total being. Bushnell thus rejected Parker's Transcendentalist position, which determined to "test" the scriptures by the authority of man's reason. In the Calvinist tradition, Bushnell maintained that man could derive full meaning from the Bible only through the grace of God's Spirit, which would act at once as revealer and interpreter of truth. The key was to understand the Bible "not as a magazine of propositions and mere dialectic entities, but as inspirations and poetic forms of life; requiring also, divine inbreathings and exaltations in us, that we may ascend into their meaning."[38]

A second norm for theological reflection to which Bushnell appealed were the creeds of the Christian church. As with the Bible, he rejected a stringent interpretation of creeds which would stifle creative work. Furthermore, no one creed was sufficient because language could never capture truth. Creeds had a history of divisiveness and dissension; this problem would be avoided if creeds were treated as summary statements of the beliefs of the faithful people rather than absolute standards of judgment. The proper role of creedal affirmation was to aid in united witness: "They are good, we rightly say, as terms of *conformity*, being the forms in which we coalesce and are comforted together."[39] Viewing creeds as guides allowing for a range of individual options allowed Bushnell to make liberal use of historic formulations. He wrote that he was able to assent "to about as many creeds as chance to fall in my way."[40]

Bushnell did, however, recognize creeds as source and guide for theology. As products of the common life, creeds reflected the Word of God as well as individual and communal experience. Creeds thus served to encapsulate the basic affirmations of Christianity to which the theologian ought repair and from which he should set forth on his constructive efforts.

A third source and guide was closely related to the creeds, yet different. One might call this third factor the tradition of the common life. Analysis will be best served through the use of an illustration. The problem of infant baptism concerned Bushnell because of his conviction that regeneration was related to participation in Christian fellowship. It is instructive to study his methodology for justifying his recommendation of infant baptism. After demonstrating close examination of scripture, comparative dogma, creeds, and history, he wrote:

> The argument may be summed up thus: beginning at a point previous, we find *customs* and *associations* that would almost certainly be issued in such a rite of family religion; in the *discourses of Christ* and the *apostolic writings* we find it actually was; and then we find the *facts of church history* correspondent.[41]

The methodology allowed a range of options for construction within a defined arena of normative assertions which were derived from multiple sources—namely, scripture, creed, tradition, and experience—all defined in reference to one another as both creative of and products of Christian community. Bushnell met with strong opposition. Liberal Boston Unitarians regarded his work as still pathetically orthodox, while both Taylorites and Tylerites charged him with opening the door for subjectivity and mysticism. Bushnell rightly appraised the situation as at base the issue of authority when he wrote that critics have charged "that I propose to throw down all the pillars of theology, break up all the solid foundations of truth, and commend every one to the liberty of his own passions, and the vagaries of his own imagination."[42] Strongly denying the charge, Bushnell insisted that, in his method, "nothing is done save simply to show how the forms in which God is offered to our faith may be *used* so as to get their true meaning and be themselves the truth to us."[43]

According to Bushnell, no one dogmatic form of God's revelation could be normative for theology. The key is the recognition that the theological methodology he proposed was inseparable from his conviction regarding the nature of religious life. The norms to which Bushnell appealed grew out of the common life he understood to be a complex reality involving the juxtaposition of individual experience and personal knowledge of God within the nurturing environment of the faithful community. Bushnell recognized that his times desperately needed a consideration of authority in religion. He struggled with the issue and sought to offer alternatives which would provide flexibility for creative work, through the immediate indwelling of God's Spirit, within a framework of authorization which he formulated as common life.

5

AUTHORITY AND THE REALITY OF SUPERNATURAL GRACE

The conception of religious authority which emerges from Bushnell's sermons, articles, and books presupposes a differentiation between a transcendent, sovereign God and his creation. This distinction was delineated most clearly in the volume *Nature and the Supernatural*. The thesis of this book is that the whole of God's creation was composed of two distinct orders or "degrees of being."[44] God certainly had not absented himself from the natural order, but neither was he wholly revealed in nature. It was Bushnell's contention that only through the imposition of supernatural grace could man come to the realization of potential regeneration. The thrust of

Nature and the Supernatural was to combat what Bushnell believed to be a dangerous and growing tendency to reject any claim to truth which could not be verified objectively by the emerging "scientific method." Bushnell did not object to science, but only to the assumption that science was an entirely adequate judge of reality. In the religious sphere, naturalism was a dominant movement in the early and mid-nineteenth century stemming from the Enlightenment and from the "age of the common man." Bushnell viewed the tendency toward naturalism with deep concern and determined that it

> must be finally arrested, by one or the other of these two methods: by restoring a distinct and properly intelligent faith in the supernatural reign of Christ such as I have undertaken to set forth, or else by a blind recoil, such as mere vacuity and the pains of vagrancy will instigate.[45]

Bushnell did not deny that common experience in the world provided clues to the nature of ultimate reality; to have attempted such a denial would have been to reject God's providential care for the universe. He did deny, however, that the intimations which occurred in the natural order could ever be sufficient to provide all raw materials required for constructive theological reflection, let alone to induce Christian faith. "There is," he argued, "no vestige of Christian life in the working-plan of nature. Christianity exists only to have a remedial action upon the contents and conditions of nature."[46]

In Bushnell's insistence on the reality of, and the need for, supernatural grace, he was much closer to Jonathan Edwards than to the liberals who would later claim to be in the tradition of the Hartford minister. Like Edwards, Bushnell perceived a gap between man's situation within the natural order and the high expectations of the Christian faith. Christianity, by definition, involved higher truth and injunctions to a higher way of life. For this reason, Bushnell objected to the assumption that science provided a methodology sufficiently inclusive to deal with all reality. A recent commentator has written that, as Bushnell saw it,

> The real threat to revealed religion posed by science, therefore, was not that of scientific discovery *per se*, but rather an unwarranted "bondage under the *method* of science": that is, the widely accepted assumption that "nothing could be true, save as it is proved by the scientific method."[47]

Rejecting neither science nor the natural, Bushnell only urged the reality of, and necessity of, a transcendent dimension. His effort was seriously misunderstood and misrepresented by interpreters. Owing to his hesitance, based on his language theory, to insist on dogmatic affirmations of doctrine, and his willingness to entertain a wide range of possible interpretations of Christianity within the authority of common life, Bushnell did in fact provide a place of beginning for liberalization within the tradition. Theodore Munger, New England preacher and theologian, became Bushnell's initial interpreter for successive generations. Munger was himself an advocate of the "new theology," which sought to find God in the natural processes of the world and which greatly elevated man's freedom and participation in his own salvation. Seeking to make Bushnell prophet and father of liberalism, Munger highlighted those aspects of *Nature and the Supernatural* which dealt with the all-encompassing providence of God over the natural order. Thus did Munger argue that Bushnell "got rid of the traditional antinomy" between nature and the supernatural and therefore "led the way into that conception of the relation of God to his world which more and more is taking possession of modern thought."[48] Munger was not wholly wrong; Bushnell always believed the entirety of creation to be God's order—his whole conception of the multiple factors of the authority of common life was based on such belief. Nevertheless, it is this partial interpretation which has informed most of the subsequent thinking and writing about Horace Bushnell.[49]

The issue is of importance for the consideration of authority because Bushnell has been regarded as one of the primary figures who prepared the way for the shift in authority which took place in American theology as the full impact of the Darwinian revolution and historical criticism began to be felt. Certainly Bushnell's work aided his followers in succeeding generations to deal in a more creative manner with the challenges and changes of the late nineteenth century than did either rigid Calvinism or liberal Unitarianism. Ironically, however, it was Bushnell's liberal *spirit*, rather than his liberal *theology*, which allowed for this modification and interpretation. The spirit emanated from his hesitance to be doctrinally dogmatic. It is a serious error to take this spirit as indicative of either a failure to account for authority or a relegation of authority to modern man's reason. Confusion may result from the fact that Bushnell's treatment of authority cannot be rigidly encapsulated; he allowed for a range of options within prescribed limits set by Bible, creeds, tradition, and individual and communal experience. Bushnell developed a position which allowed both for continuity within the bounds of Christian tradition and change in a time of confusion and uncertainty.

CHAPTER III

AUTHORITY AND SCIENTIFIC REASON: WILLIAM ADAMS BROWN

1

SOCIAL AND INTELLECTUAL DISLOCATION AND THE CRISIS OF THEOLOGICAL AUTHORITY

Horace Bushnell did not live to see the renewal and stability he hoped would follow the Civil War in America; his death in 1876 came in the midst of a period of severe social and intellectual dislocation. In the last half of the nineteenth century, America underwent sustained and rapid change. Animosity between North and South continued and was exacerbated by the economic progress enjoyed by the North and denied to the South. The national picture was characterized by a tendency toward technological advance, urbanization, and disparateness of wealth.

The war provided a significant boost to technology in the North. A nation traditionally rural became rapidly urban as the growing number of urban industrial workers could be provided for by a fewer number of farmers. Industrialists were praised for offering weary farm workers an escape from rural drudgery to the factories of the cities. The horrors of urban slums and the sacrifice of persons to industrial development were neither anticipated nor understood. Enormous amounts of money were accumulated by ingenuity, management skills, and luck; the vast empires in steel, railroads, oil, and banking offered an open field for the inventor and the manipulator. Business and industry grew to unprecedented importance as consolidation and new techniques of management became necessary to serve a national market made possible by the burgeoning railroad. The United States, however, had no conceptual tools with which to perceive what was happening.

The benefits of the new technology and increased wealth were not filtering out to the masses. The inequality of the distribution of goods was not lost on the workers, but workers had few ideas about how to redress the imbalance, and owners saw no difference between the new technological business complexes and the old individualistic, entrepreneurial traditions of the small-town agricultural existence. As one recent interpreter writes, "The United States in the nineteenth century offered a peculiarly inviting field for coarse leadership and crudely exercised power."[1] Bloody strikes and riots which killed many people and left a permanent blot on the history of the nation occurred in 1877, 1886, 1892, and 1894. The decades prior to the turn of the century also witnessed a great increase in immigration, and the influx of foreign peoples did nothing to settle the uncertainties of the nation.

Even as industrialization, immigration, and urbanization engendered unrest and disorder in the society, intellectual breakthroughs which challenged traditional assumptions about man and his world undermined both popular and scholarly convictions about the meaning of life and created an unsettled intellectual climate. Undoubtedly the publication, in 1859, of Darwin's *The Origin of Species* was the seminal scholarly achievement of the century. The heated debates which took place first among scientists and intellectuals and then among popularizers in the half century after the publication of Darwin's volume testify to recognition that the theory challenged not only previous scientific assumptions and familiar understandings of the Bible and religion but also the familiar conceptions of the place of man himself in the order of living creatures. *The Origin of Species* had a profound impact on the whole range of American intellectual life in the late nineteenth century as scientists were joined by social thinkers, religionists, ethicists, and philosophers in the debate about the truth and meaning of evolution.

Darwin's breakthrough greatly boosted the growing interest in the methodological procedures of scientific discovery, which was not confined to investigation of natural, physical reality but was being attempted in history and even applied to society and economy. Suddenly science seemed to be man's hope; it became the standard by which all endeavor might be judged. As one historian observes, "Science was the idol of opinion, and no interdict sacred or temporal stunted its growth."[2] The effects of the new enthusiasm for science were various; two of the most interesting outgrowths of the basic Darwinian insight in terms of popular culture were social Darwinism and the "gospel of wealth."

Social Darwinism grew out of inaccurate application of Darwin's principles to the social sphere. Herbert Spencer, the English philosopher, used biological concepts, especially natural selection, to explain relationships within society. Spencer and his disciples argued that the state should stay entirely out of economic affairs; progress could be realized only if the weak were naturally destroyed and the fit were allowed to survive. The doctrines of social Darwinism were congenial to the rugged individual competition of late-nineteenth-century America.

Coupled with the individualism of evangelicalism and the American democratic faith in the free individual, social Darwinism produced the "gospel of wealth." This popular set of beliefs taught that men were meant to achieve wealth, that the good man would succeed, that wealth implied responsibility, and that the state should maintain order, protect property, and otherwise leave economic affairs to those who were "naturally selected" for leadership and control.[3] A great many churchmen, including important ministers of the day, subscribed enthusiastically to the doctrines of the "gospel of wealth." In 1901, William Lawrence, Episcopal Bishop of Massachusetts, wrote an article in which he asserted, "Now we are in a position to affirm that neither history, experience, nor the Bible necessarily sustains the common distrust of the effect of material wealth on morality. . . . Godliness is in league with riches."[4]

The easy equation of godliness and riches, along with the unsettled social and intellectual climate of the last quarter of the nineteenth century, caused some in the church to recognize that both new formulations of the Christian message and new institutional patterns for the life of the church were needed. The response of churchmen took two primary forms; one had to do with the social and reform aspects of Christianity, and the other with intellectual constructs.

Social reformers, popularly referred to as "Social Gospelers," became convinced that Christianity, rightly interpreted in terms of the man Jesus, was a profound revolutionary force for social justice. Washington Gladden, Charles M. Sheldon, Richard T. Ely, and Walter Rauschenbusch were among the leaders who sought to make the kingdom of God real in the world. The active span of the Social Gospel movement in America was roughly between the years 1870 and 1920.[5]

As social Darwinism and the "gospel of wealth" demonstrated the need for the redefinition of the church's mission which resulted in the Social Gospel, so popular conceptions of the impact of Darwin's scientific hypothesis and empirical methodology brought on an attempt by some theologians to construct an explication of the

Christian message that would be compatible with, or at least take account of, the new scientific mind-set. Although some theologians, like B. B. Warfield, held tenaciously to traditional orthodoxy, and some, like Gerald Birney Smith, abandoned all attempts at reconciling new ideas with old, others, notably William Adams Brown, tried the middle course, seeking both faithfulness to Christian tradition and serious encounter with modern developments.[6]

The attempt to express the Christian faith in such a way that it would be meaningful in an age enamored with science was, in part at least, an apologetic effort. At a time when the faith was under fire, liberal theologians and clergy sought to shift the ground on which they stood in order to claim that their legitimacy was based not on that which the critics were attacking but on something altogether different and far more justifiable, namely, the improvement of man's earthly condition. At the initiation of the apologetic task, the question of authority becomes crucial.

William Adams Brown believed that the central theological problem of his time was that of authority. One's choice among the perplexing new currents of thought and new recommendations for the social order, he felt, was dependent on one's view of religious authority. Brown identified three themes which always engage the attention of religious thinkers. The first was authority, the second God, the third salvation. The theologian's first and most abiding question, however, was the location of authority; this was so because the nature and seat of religious authority determined one's entire approach to theology. Therefore, while modern theology needed to retain the richness of the Protestant tradition, it also needed to engage itself seriously with modern science so that, through the adaptation of concepts of scientific methodology, it might achieve authorization meaningful to modern man.

2

A PATRICIAN IN THEOLOGY

William Adams Brown (1865-1943) was the scion of a wealthy, intellectual, and distinguished New York family. He was educated at St. Paul's School and Yale College before going, in 1888, to Union Seminary. Union, which was founded in 1836 by a group of New School Presbyterians, "was unique among the religious schools of its day for its combination of scholarly interests and catholic spirit."[7] Brown had natural ties to Union. His mother's father, William Adams, a prominent New York Presbyterian minister, was the first president of the faculty, and his Grandfather Brown, a Wall Street financier and shipping magnate, was a generous contributor to the seminary and a member of its Board of Trustees. An excellent student, Brown received the seminary's graduate fellowship, which he used for travel to Berlin, where he studied under Adolf Harnack and Julius Kaftan.

Brown's sophisticated background made him unusually susceptible to the problems Harnack and Kaftan were exploring; both Ritschlians, they sought new ways to make the truth of Jesus Christ meaningful for enlightened contemporary life. Intellectually, Brown found himself unable to accept a traditional orthodoxy, and he early decided that his career should be built on the effort to relate the gospel to the needs of modern man. Harnack and Kaftan convinced him that a redefinition of the gospel was possible without the loss of its essence. Harnack struck Brown as the epitome of "what a teacher of religion should be"; the young American student sat under the renowned church historian for two years and was enthralled. "I have heard many great lecturers," he later wrote, "but Harnack was the only man whom I could hear for two hours a day for six days in the week, for two years, and at the end, look forward as eagerly to the last lecture as to the first." Less famous than Harnack, Julius Kaftan was the systematic theologian of Ritschlianism. Brown judged him "too little appreciated."[8]

Brown essentially adopted Kaftan's articulation of the task and problem of theology and built upon it his own statement of modern theology. Kaftan maintained that authority was the most important principle of theology. According to Kaftan, men need authority in order to live their lives; and authority, by definition, has a quality apart from man's personal judgment. "The distinguishing characteristic of authority is its independence of the personal judgment and liking of those with whom it has to do."[9] The importance of authority is that it is self-authenticating and "has validity because it is valid."[10] While Kaftan made authority *independent* of man's subjective judgment, he did not make it wholly *external* to man. True authority gains the consent of the individual conscience and is, indeed, "inwardly recognized and self-containing."[11] Kaftan rejected both the hierarchical external authority of the Roman Catholic Church and what he claimed to be the equally external authority of biblical infallibility propounded by the Reformers.[12] Attempting to retain the self-authenticating nature of authority and the ingredients of inner appropriation and self-containment, Kaftan proposed that divine revelation, understood as a communication of truth which demands and elicits willing obedience, constituted authority for the Protestant.

The influence of Kaftan on Brown is unmistakable. In many ways, Brown's theology was a perpetual reworking, albeit in a creative way, of the basic problem to which he was introduced by Julius Kaftan. Brown accepted Kaftan's notion that revelation was authority. According to Brown, Jesus Christ was both the manner and the content of man's knowledge of God. As will be demonstrated, however, the definition of revelation propounded was designed to allow for Brown's operative authority, which was man's reason.

3

TOWARD A THEOLOGY FOR MODERN MAN

Upon his return from Berlin, Brown was appointed to teach church history at Union Seminary. In 1902, he published a historical study entitled *The Essence of Christianity* in which he attempted to establish a definition of Christianity which would be compatible with the findings and methodology of the new science. Brown's effort was organized around the problem that, although Christianity claims to be absolute, believers have consistently disagreed over competing, or even contradictory, interpretations of the nature of the Absolute. Though he did not use the word explicitly, the issue clearly was authority: How was one to know *which* interpretation of Christianity was correct?

Brown constructed a typology accounting for three views of the Absolute. The first view, which he called "ontological," was one where the Absolute was understood to be completely independent of finite existence, a supernatural being sharply distinguished from the world. Adherents to what Brown called the "mathematical" position regarded the Absolute as a limiting reality. The analogy was to the mathematical infinite; thus, in this second position, man could have no real knowledge of the Absolute. A third position, which Brown referred to as "psychological," understood the Absolute as participant in the entirety of experience and existence, the ultimate reality which provides meaning and order for all life in the world.[13]

Kaftan's position on authority, and Brown's own shaping of the problem in the first chapter of *The Essence of Christianity*, became the basis for Brown's theological thinking throughout his life. He subsequently attributed the "ontological" position to Roman Catholicism or Protestant orthodoxy, the "mathematical" to radical liberalism, and the "psychological" to his own restatement of the gospel, which he called "modern theology" and systematically set forth in 1906 in his classic *Christian Theology in Outline*, published thirteen years after he had assumed the chair of systematic theology at Union.[14]

The surging feeling of optimism which infused intellectual man's view of himself in the America of the first decades of the twentieth century is difficult to overestimate. New methods of historical and scientific study questioned age-old convictions. Under the assumption that man had the right of endorsement or rejection, all authority was reexamined. Only a theologian who barricaded himself from the world could escape doing a fundamental reconsideration of traditional claims. William Adams Brown was much affected by the spirit of his times, yet he was also convinced that Christianity could not be reduced to a scientific methodology wholly without remainder. Brown sought not to reduce Christianity to science but to demonstrate the compatibility of the two. There was, in Christianity, an unmistakable element which stood apart from man's subjective inclination. The totality of Brown's theological work was an attempt to explicate Christianity's self-authenticating authority, which he saw to be juxtaposed between the enduring tradition of the faith and the perpetually new realities of the present.

According to Brown, the task of theology was to interpret the gospel for modern men in such a way as ever to embrace both continuity and change. He always recognized the difficulty of such an effort but did not shrink from the challenge. The tradition had to be preserved, but it also had to be applied to the present; indeed, he argued, "the office of Christian theology is not fully accomplished until it has fulfilled this double task."[15] Essentially, Brown endeavored to modify the nature of the authority of Christianity in such a way as to harmonize it with contemporary thought. An examination of some key elements of his theology demonstrates the salient features of his total product.

The *God* of whom William Adams Brown wrote was *immanent* rather than wholly separate from the world. God, acting through human beings, was a part of historical development and reality. Opposed to the radical discontinuity posited by traditional orthodoxy, Brown rejected the distinction between natural and supernatural reality as cumbersome and false in an age of science. Science appeared to countermand earlier assumptions that a supernatural realm existed apart from the empirically verifiable natural order. One answer was to telescope the two and thus eliminate the problem. It

44

could then be argued that belief in God required affirmation of nothing other than worldly phenomena. Thus Brown maintained that "God is permanently present in the world in the laws which direct his activity and which express his character; that is, he is immanent."[16]

The characteristic liberal notion of continuity became most important in a consideration of how and what man knew of God. The transcendent sovereignty, mystery, and independence of Calvin's God, so seemingly incongruous with scientific sophistication, was banished from the liberal's theology. Brown perceived God's presence in all the wonders man experienced, from the "tiniest atom" to "the farthest star"; but above all, God's "wise, loving, and holy purpose" was active in *man's own best self*.[17]

The assumption of the doctrine of continuity was that man was sufficient and able to be on rather intimate terms with the Deity. "Modern theology" shifted the emphasis from God and his purposes to man and his world. For this reason, *Jesus Christ* occupied the place of *primary theological significance* for William Adams Brown. It was in Jesus that Brown found the singularly absolute nature of Christianity. Through Jesus, God revealed himself; in Jesus, man might experience what it was truly to be a man; and in Jesus' teachings, man might find normative guidance for individual and corporate life.

Brown rejected the idea that God became man and dwelt on earth in the form of Jesus. Rather, in the man Jesus, God's spirit and presence became fully realized and manifest. The subtle difference was crucial. The emphasis in Brown's writing was on the man Jesus rather than on God. The doctrine of incarnation meant that God, who had always been active in human history, found full expression in Jesus of Nazareth. Brown therefore did not have to concern himself with Jesus' origin or the complex problems of messianic consciousness. Jesus was fully human and demonstrated the perfect indwelling of God in man. Rational man could empirically verify at least the outward elements of Jesus' life; this fact was significant because, according to Brown, it provided a meaningful historical foundation for faith.

Man's experience of the truth of Jesus' life and teachings was the conclusive evidence for his understanding of God. Brown began with man, and the man Jesus, and moved to God. The reason for thus proceeding was to allow the theologian to claim that man had—in his own experience—what amounted to scientific evidence in matters religious. Brown summarized his methodology in a crucial passage which deserves close scrutiny:

45

What God is in himself we cannot say, and it is futile to inquire. Hence, any attempt to construct the person of Christ by the aid of abstract conceptions like the Absolute, or the Logos, which have no basis in *experience*, is to invite failure. The true *task of the theologian is to study the human Jesus*, that he may learn from an analysis of his life and work what are the features of his character and ministry which give him his unique power to uplift and transform human life. When we have done this we shall have learned how it comes to pass that in him *we find that practical power to help which we call God.*[18]

Methodologically, at least, God was relegated to second place by Brown. Jesus was crucial because he alone, through his earthly ministry, made possible man's knowledge of God.

Brown's doctrine of God and his understanding of Jesus Christ led him naturally to a very *high anthropology*. No hint of pessimism about man's condition is to be found in Brown's writings. Rejecting the idea of original sin, Brown affirmed that man had the potential progressively to achieve even the ideal of Jesus.[19] Man's sin was selfishness, which was the failure to act according to Jesus' teachings. Man overcame his sin when, through revelation, he realized the truth of Jesus' teachings and sought to appropriate them in his life. Salvation came as man understood that he *could* and *ought* to live up to Jesus' example. Brown really regarded Jesus as the epitome of man, and this emphasis was the key to his understanding of God, man, and authority.[20]

Brown was convinced that all of life was perpetually moving toward the ultimate goal of the kingdom of God. In matters of faith and commitment as well as community and social order, he understood *progress* to be a fundamental principle. Against the sudden conversion experience, like that of the apostle Paul, Brown maintained that gradual conversion through a progressive appropriation of the truths of Jesus was better suited to modern educational philosophy. Insisting that Jesus himself emphasized "growth" in faith rather than "sudden and dramatic conversion," Brown suggested that "advocates of the new education feel at home in this language."[21] The fact that modern educational theory was congenial to his position was important to Brown. He consistently sought to make his theology acceptable to modern thought.

The progressive nature of growth in faith was inherent, according to Brown, in God's nature; it was for this reason that he rejected the idea of the once-for-all revelation taught by orthodoxy. Knowledge of

God was progressively appropriated. He maintained that God's "final word to man is to be sought in the present and in the future rather than in the past."[22] Brown wrote further that the totality of the world's events was teleological in nature, but progress toward God's end was not without confusion and setback. Evil, tragedy, and apparent regression were incorporated into the totality of God's teleology in which conflict and struggle were ingredient.[23]

The affirmation of a steady, gradual, progressive realization of the perfect order was much in line with the general optimism which accompanied early scientific breakthroughs during an era in which genuine improvement in many areas of life could be documented. The doctrine of progress grew directly out of Brown's desire to emphasize, in his "modern theology," those aspects of Christianity which most directly and most practicably concerned man's life in the world.

4

AUTHORITY AND MAN'S REASON

In order to understand precisely the nature of Brown's notion of authority, it will be helpful to see the way in which he dealt with approaches to authority characteristic of Christianity.

Brown regarded the Bible as permanently authoritative for the Christian because it contained the necessary ingredients of God's revelation in Jesus Christ. But when Brown wrote that the Bible was authoritative, he did not mean that it was *the* authority. Departing from the dominant position within American Presbyterianism, Brown heartily endorsed biblical criticism, believing that its sophisticated scientific method made the Bible more useful to modern men. The Bible was written by men inspired by God, but the emphasis was on "men," which meant that, for Brown, no simple doctrine of infallibility—or, as he preferred, "inerrancy"—would do. He admitted that the Bible was unique, but he insisted that it was a human book to be studied and interpreted like other literature.[24]

Brown was convinced that, if properly studied, the Bible would yield increasingly helpful information about Jesus Christ. In what was a circular argument, Brown affirmed that the Bible was important because it was the best source for information about Jesus. Yet Jesus was the criterion by which the value of the Bible's witness was judged. The Bible, he wrote, "is the book which gives us the most direct, reliable, and first-hand knowledge of Jesus Christ, the founder, the standard, and the renewer of the Christian religion."[25] The Bible functions, then, as a common guide to the Christian faith for believers. Providing common language and experience for the faithful, it is "at once a revelation and the record of a revelation."[26]

Brown thus made a distinction between something which is authoritative and that which is *the* authority. The Bible was author-itative, but it could not be *the* authority because it was open to too many diverse interpretations. Only if it spoke univocally in such a way that a myriad of positions would be disallowed could it be ultimately authoritative. Brown thought that the position of biblical infallibility held by some Protestants was nonsense and flew in the face of the fact "that the Bible had not done what an infallible book is expected to do. It has not given its message in such clear and unmistakable form that all Christians have agreed as to its mean-ing."[27] Variegated and sometimes self-contradictory, the Bible pro-vided no clear inner standard of self-judgment; it simply could not be finally authoritative for modern scientific consciousness.

Although *Theology in Outline* included very few pages dealing with the church, Brown was always concerned about, and dedicated to, the church, which he understood to be the human community of those who were seeking to live according to the example of Jesus Christ and to perpetuate the broadening influence of Jesus in the world. The church was the community of worship, but primarily for Brown it was the *teaching agent* of the Christian faith. In this sense it was authoritative as any teacher is authoritative; but it was not, and could not be, *the* authority. Brown's strongest objection to Roman Catholicism was in regard to the nature of church authority. In its teaching function, Brown believed, "the church tells us the story of what Jesus has meant to all the generations which have come after him."[28] The church could not, however, claim to be the unique mediate authority because it was preeminently a human community and, as such, subject to error as well as other human foibles and follies. Brown recognized, as had Bushnell, that the Christian community could never assert absolute ascendancy over the individual conscience. He always insisted that, in a conflict between conviction and the teaching of the church, the Protestant had to follow his conscience even if it meant breaking with the church.[29]

Brown sought to find an alternative to traditional approaches to authority which would avoid the shortcomings he found in them. In his book *Pathways to Certainty*, he sorted out four ways by which judgment might be made among conflicting theological claims. Brown's categories were *authority*, or the way of the witness of the church or Bible;[30] *reasoning*, the use of the logic of the mind to test hypotheses; *intuition*, the way of feeling or inner experience; and *experiment*, the testing of hypotheses in the practical affairs of life.

The conclusion was that none of the four ways was adequate; the Christian needed to make use of *all four ways* if he were to arrive at certainty.[31] No one of the paths, Brown insisted, could stand up under the joint demands of the Protestant tradition and scientific methodology, the two fundamental criteria of "modern theology." The four together, however, at once satisfied the requirement of Protestant tradition, because they were traditional norms, *and* the requirement of scientific methodology, because man's reason was to adjudicate among the four alternatives. In fact by calling upon man's intellect in such a way, Brown asserted the primary authority of reason.

Brown objected to the traditional approaches to religious authority because they presumed to *impose* upon man external normative standards. External imposition grated with the notion of science, which put a premium on self-discovery and knowledge achieved experimentally and experientially. Persuaded that it was not necessary for man to subjugate his intellectual abilities in order to realize the truth of Christianity, Brown believed that *man's mind* and *reason* had to be satisfied if true appropriation of Christianity were to be realized. Such an approach is significantly different from that taken in the epistemological theories of Jonathan Edwards and Horace Bushnell, for whom man's reason could not be finally authoritative for theological reflection. Their conviction was that man's knowledge of God was dependent on God's immediate revelation of himself to man's heart. Matters of the mind were not unimportant, but they were secondary and unable to induce faith.

Brown accepted the judgment of early scientific and historical criticism that man's reason was sufficient to judge the adequacy of propositions according to their ability to make sense of modern experience. In *The Harvard Theological Review*, Brown wrote, "Our primary reason for accepting the new theology is intellectual. We hold it because it explains the facts of life as a whole better than the old."[32] This quotation is the key to Brown's notion of authority. Man's rational capacity is assumed. The new theology is not self-authenticating but "acceptable"; Jesus is authoritative because he, through his earthly ministry, made himself acceptable to man, and because he mediated enlightenment. Salvation thus presupposed "right knowledge."

Writing of modern democratic men, Brown put the matter baldly: "If they are to have a God, it must be one whom they have *tried for themselves* and found *satisfying*."[33] Even the hint of man judging his God was heretical to Protestant orthodoxy. For Brown, man's choice of his God seemed to be made according to the criterion of intellectual satisfaction.

Brown was contradictory in his attempt to satisfy both scientific method and Protestant tradition. Ultimate authority, which he understood to be Jesus Christ, was in some sense self-authenticating and irresistible. Yet, at the same time, it authenticated itself to the individual's intellect in such a way that it ordered and made sense of his life and thus received his willing consent.[34] Brown insisted that subjectivity did not inevitably follow from the assertion that man's experience was the seat of authority.

The skeptic might maintain that Brown simply wanted to have it both ways. In part, such an analysis is true; but nevertheless he was pushing at something profound. God, as he manifested himself to man in Jesus Christ, was the objective standard; but he was authoritative only insofar as man did in fact experience him and come into communion with his manifestation. Man's experience of authority was not merely subjective, it was also objective because it had an objective ground.[35] The ultimate thus became man's subjective appropriation of God's objective self-manifestation, which was, of course, Jesus Christ. Jesus Christ was the objective authority for the Christian, but Jesus Christ was always subjectively grounded in the faithful experience of the believer.

Brown sought an objective authority to which Bible, church, experience, and reason all pointed yet which was subjectively grounded in man. Jesus Christ alone sufficiently met Brown's criteria to serve as authority for faith and order. Brown placed his emphasis on Jesus because he felt that the historic reality of Jesus allowed for the application of scientific method to constructive theology. The Christian's concept of God was arrived at by examining the way in which Jesus spoke of God, one's concept of man according to the way Jesus treated man, one's concept of society and the way life should be lived by the way Jesus lived and taught.[36]

William Adams Brown always sought to "read the mind of Jesus" as he worked out his theological positions. Turning repeatedly to the synoptic historical records, Brown based many judgments on the way Jesus acted. But Brown was not restricted to biblical accounts; he felt the "mind of Christ" also revealed itself in man's individual and group experiences. Jesus thus functioned as norm for both theology and Christian life. The contemporary tendency to divide systematic theology and Christian ethics never would have received the approval of Brown. There was no chair of ethics at Union while he was Roosevelt Professor, and he always emphasized the practical applicability of theological reflection. Never was he content to do theology apart from ethics; to divide the two was unthinkable.

The reason for Brown's refusal to distinguish between theology and ethics was that he was serious about Jesus as norm. A failure to ground theological reflection in the practical affairs of men was to deviate from Jesus' authority. If anything was true of Jesus, it was that he acted on his principles; he lived out his life before God caring for men, exemplifying the best in man.[37] It was Jesus' manhood which made his authority conclusive. The emphasis on Jesus' humanity permitted Brown to allow the possibility that another man could be like Jesus and that all men should try to be like Jesus.[38] One did not understand true authority unless he sought to implement Jesus' commands; present-day disciples were expected, as were the original twelve, to be like Jesus: "After nineteen centuries, we still look to him as our example. To us, as to the first disciples, he is not only true man, but ideal man."[39]

According to Brown, then, three key elements informed any consideration of true religious authority. The first of these was that true authority was not simply imposed from without but irresistibly appealed to man's inner conscience and elicited his consent. In a profound way, true authority was *internal*; but it was not subjective. Secondly, religious authority was objective and *absolute*. Brown struggled at length with the problem of the absolute. He was not willing to accept a relativism that subjected Christianity to one among many valid religious expressions. Appealing to philosophical and historical evidence, Brown argued that no violence was done to human intellect and reason in the affirmation that Jesus was the epitome of religious thought and action and as such was absolutely authoritative for man.

The third element constitutive of religious authority was its *ethical* dimension. Religious authority had to do with the way one's life was to be led. Definitive and practical norms for man's personal and corporate life were set forth in Jesus' life and teachings. Not only was Jesus authoritative for the individual Christian, he had normative significance for the entire society. Jesus could function as authority for society because, in him, men could be lifted out of themselves into the perspective of the good of the whole. Indeed, Brown argued that God's purpose in history was *primarily* social; the training of the individual was designed to prepare him for participation in the kingdom of God toward which society was progressively moving.[40]

The goal was enhanced as men accepted Jesus as authority and helped others to understand his teachings and put them into practice.

In his earlier works, Brown suggested that the kingdom of God was normative for society and progressively being realized but would not be fully attained in the world.[41] Later, with the publication of *Beliefs That Matter* and especially *Is Christianity Practicable?*, Brown affirmed the possibility of the realization of the kingdom on earth. If man conceivably could become as Jesus, then it stood to reason that the perfect society was at least a possibility.[42] "It may take time. It may take patience. We may not live to see it. Our children may not live to see it. But in the end it will be done."[43] Again with reference to the kingdom, he wrote that "we have seen no reason to doubt that it can be realized in fact, if all who believe in this ideal cooperate to bring it about."[44]

Just as Brown's argument in regard to Jesus as authority was weakened through his appeal to man's intellectual capacities for justification, so was his assertion that Jesus was authoritative for society weakened through his appeal to the needs of a cooperative society for justification. Men in community, he argued, needed an organizing principle to which mutual assent could be given, thereby providing for internal coherence. Adherence to the teachings of Jesus would allow men to transcend themselves and accept a common integrative norm. The argument was pragmatic; it was based on the assumption that if true brotherhood were to be achieved, there must be a common set of principles, a rule or norm, to test personal claims and to counteract tendencies toward individualism.[45] Brown's attempt to justify authority on grounds of social utility was to make, once again, man's judgment of his needs authoritative.

Brown's theology sought to make it possible for men immersed in modern consciousness to tap the deep resources of the Christian tradition. The theoretical argument that internal appropriation of authority does not necessarily imply subjectivity seeks to explicate one of the profound truths of Christianity: namely, that God's authority is objective yet elicits, in an irresistible way, man's willing consent. Brown constantly negates the inherent strength of his position, however, by including statements to satisfy modernists. His affirmation that the "primary reason for accepting the new theology is intellectual," for instance, places *man's intellect* as judge of the reasonableness of a theological proposition; and modern man becomes the authority. Though he makes a constructive and important effort, Brown never sufficiently reconciles the objective authority of Jesus

Christ with the "reasonableness" of modern science. It remains to be seen whether Jesus-as-authority can ever be reasonable in terms of scientific methodology.

Between Bushnell and Brown, the important intellectual and social changes discussed earlier in this study literally shifted the grounds upon which authority could be discussed. Affirmations with regard to the Bible, for instance, taken for granted by Edwards and Bushnell, were now frontally challenged. These social realities brought about a completely new notion of authority. Notice, however, that though the grounds shifted and the issues were new, the fundamental problem was the perennial one: In a time of social and intellectual disorder and confusion, the key issue for Protestant theology is authority for theological reflection and ethical prescription.

CHAPTER IV

AUTHORITY AND REVELATION: H. RICHARD NIEBUHR

1

A NEW ORDERING OF AUTHORITY FOR THEOLOGY

The theological position articulated by William Adams Brown throughout his life varied little from the system he set forth in *Christian Theology in Outline* in 1906. Although he lived until 1943, Brown's basic liberal theology, including his answer to the problem of authority, remained constant. Amidst the currents of political, social, and theological change which swirled about him, Brown channeled most of his energies into emerging international ecumenical efforts and practical matters of church and society. Brown's unwillingness to allow the multiple crises of the first half of the twentieth century to affect his theology was not characteristic, however, of a young crop of theologians—among whom the Niebuhr brothers were outstanding—who, long before Brown's death, would offer a fresh reconstruction. In particular, H. Richard Niebuhr would wrestle with the recurrent theme of authority in theology and find his home among those of his American ancestors for whom the attempt to account for religious authority opened the door to a revitalized Christian theology.

Although no two liberal theological positions of the early twentieth century were exactly alike, a basic characteristic was the acceptance of man's reason as an important authoritative judge of Christian theology.[1] Therefore, liberalism tended to emphasize the ethical value of theological claims because humanitarian concerns could more easily be made "reasonable" than traditional doctrines. An evangelical liberal like William Adams Brown, for instance, sought to articulate doctrines in terms of ethical norms and thus legitimate theology by demonstrating its "social good"; theology was "a way of expressing in appropriate categories the meaning and value of the moral experience of God."[2] The assumption was that scientific reason could observe, describe, and evaluate the extent to which theology aided individual and corporate moral life.

A shift in dominant understandings of authority for theology in the third and fourth decades of the twentieth century may be attributable to a growing sense that liberal assumptions about man's reasonableness and humanitarian instincts were descriptively in error. World War I, a shattering blow to many liberals, was followed by years of continued urbanization, technological advance, cultural diversification, and increased mobility. America had just prepared physically and psychologically for the war when it ended; a great deal of latent energy found its release in the excess and confusion of the postwar twenties as Americans sought to recapture the past and eliminate the unpleasantness of the war experience through group action and legislative statute. Both conservative and liberal factions of Protestantism proved inadequate to meet the demands of the time.

In a pathetic effort to stem the tide of what they perceived to be moral decay, the fundamentalists staged their rendezvous with modernism in Dayton, Tennessee, in July of 1925. The theory of evolution, they feared, would weaken religion and thus, almost certainly, individual and social morality. Fear of the impact of urban centers and "city life-styles" on the morality of the nation also caused many main-line Protestant churches to join fundamentalists in the fight for Prohibition.[3]

Some churchmen uncritically accommodated themselves to the ethic of individual acquisitiveness which attributed positive value to unending varieties of business endeavor. This attitude was epitomized by the publication, in 1925, of Bruce Barton's best-selling volume *The Man Nobody Knows*, in which Jesus was pictured as a model businessman.[4] Many Christians found the answer to the problem of Christ and culture by equating the two.

Liberal theologians distinguished themselves from both fundamentalists and those who equated Christ and culture. However, owing to their basic affirmation of man's potential, ability, and reason, liberals had little conception of an authority for theology which might stand over against man in opposition to the reactionary or accommodationist theological positions which proliferated, playing havoc with the independence and integrity of the church in America. Sidney Mead is probably close to the mark in observing, "If the theology of the fundamentalists was archaic and anachronistic, that of the liberals was secularized and innocuous."[5] The coming of severe economic depression in 1929 shattered the buoyancy implicit in the prosperity of the twenties and contributed to the intellectual regrouping which was to have a profound impact on theology. In the early thirties, liberal theology, as a structured system of beliefs and teachings, the theology of the American establishment for many decades, disintegrated.[6] Some significant theological reconstruction was necessary.

One source of help lay in the important currents of Continental thought, a story so familiar that it need not be recounted here. European theology had never been without doubters who were profoundly uncomfortable with liberalism. Søren Kierkegaard and Peter Taylor Forsyth, both in different ways, ably questioned liberal assumptions, but the time was most ripe when Karl Barth published *Der Römerbrief* in 1918. Barth's critique made great impact in Europe during the twenties and by the thirties was transfusing new blood into American theological veins. Undoubtedly the climate of theological opinion on the Continent had an important role in shaping the nature and direction of theological reconstruction in America.

This study has already demonstrated, however, that the native roots of the post-liberal thinking, like that which emerged in America in the mid-thirties, run very deep indeed.[7] The new ordering of theological authority which accompanied the disintegration of liberalism was not unlike the shifts in thinking about authority which preceded the efforts at theological reconstruction on the part of Jonathan Edwards and Horace Bushnell. Static and accommodative theology needed the revitalization that came only from new openness to God's transcendent reality.

2

TOWARD THE INDEPENDENCE OF THE CHURCH

Few families have contributed more conspicuously to theological studies than that into which Helmut Richard Niebuhr was born on September 3, 1894, in Wright City, Missouri. Son of a minister of the Evangelical Synod of North America, Richard Niebuhr was early steeped in the theology and life-style of the German Reformed tradition, which coupled an appreciation for learning with evangelical piety. Niebuhr was graduated from Elmhurst College in 1912, a little school related to his church located in what was then a small suburban village west of Chicago. His ministerial training was completed at Eden Theological Seminary in 1915 and he was ordained the next year, when he became pastor of a congregation in St. Louis. While serving his church, Niebuhr earned the M.A. degree at Washington University before returning as teacher to Eden Seminary, where he taught until 1922, when he began his studies at Yale Divinity School; he received the Ph.D in 1924. Niebuhr was president of Elmhurst College and taught again at Eden Seminary before he took up the long career of teaching at Yale University which was to span thirty-one years, until his death in 1962.

Richard's brother Reinhold exerted greater immediate influence and was better known. The most far-reaching influence of Richard Niebuhr was in the classroom, where he trained scores of Protestant ministers for America and many distinguished teachers of religion and theology. Indeed, the influence of Richard Niebuhr can be understood only if one considers the subtle but crucial impact he had on a generation of theological scholars who have in turn determined the shape of the discipline for several decades. Precisely because he did not concern himself primarily with his immediate situation but with timeless themes of theological significance, Richard Niebuhr's influence has endured. The nature and quality of his scholarly writings are such that they continue to be fresh and important in the process of theological reflection.

Niebuhr developed facility in German in the Reformed parsonage in which he was reared and was thus able to expose himself to important thinking being done in the German university centers. His Yale Ph.D dissertation, "Ernst Troeltsch's Philosophy of Religion," was an explication of Troeltsch's thought. The primary issue, as Niebuhr saw it, was Troeltsch's emphasis on the impossibility of extricating oneself from historical immediacy. Evaluations and decisions, he believed, no matter how reasoned or thoughtful, could in no sense be interpreted as universally final or absolute; a fundamental relativism was at the base of man's experience because he was a historical being. At the same time, this relativism did not mean that all value and obligation were relative; within a relative setting, absolute value was not only plausible but actual. Values were relative, then, to their historical situation, yet within a particular situation they were absolutely obligatory.[8]

Troeltsch's philosophy seemed to undercut Christianity's historical claim to unique and absolute truth. The core issue of Troeltsch's work, according to Niebuhr, had to do with the authority of Christianity: "The center and the theme of his work became the problem of the absoluteness of Christianity in view of the historical relativisation of all religion."[9] The problem of authority for theology and the moral life which Niebuhr identified in Troeltsch's work became the organizing problem and enduring issue for his own career of theological study and writing.[10] What claims could be made for particular theological articulations? Furthermore, how did these claims translate from the realms of philosophy and theology into the historical immediacy of ethical action without falling prey to a relativism destined to make them innocuous or irrelevant?

In the late twenties, the relativism of Christian institutions and claims seemed particularly evident in America. Coupling sociological and historical tools with the Troeltschian insight he had gained in his dissertation, Niebuhr produced a keen analysis of American churches in *The Social Sources of Denominationalism*. In this volume, published in the apocalyptic year 1929, Niebuhr examined the functional role of religion in any society and demonstrated the sociological forces which determined church policy in matters of both theology and polity.

Niebuhr's brilliant analysis unmasked pretension and manifested the church's subjection to the social order. Examining the sociological realities of the history of the American church, Niebuhr pointed to the way in which churches were formed according to social class, geographical location, economic development, and patterns of urbanization and immigration. Invariably, Niebuhr found that church positions, decisions, and growth could be accounted for on the basis of nontheological factors. This subjugation of theological norm was particularly evident with regard to racial separatism. Throughout American history, churches had compromised biblical teaching and church tradition to justify racial segregation and a separate denominational life for black Christians.

The issue of authority hovered under the surface of the volume. Sociological analysis demonstrated that social forces were, to a significant degree, the authoritative determinants of the church's life. Prior assumptions, with regard to race, for instance, determined scholarly theological writings which were, in turn, used to justify racial separatism in the churches. Priority for both theological reflection and ethical prescription was given to penultimate factors of human social existence. Having contributed this path-breaking analysis, it was not surprising that Richard Niebuhr should have been among the vanguard of young theologians in America calling upon the church, in the midst of the thirties, to distinugish itself from the world and assert its distinctive message. The small book which he wrote with Wilhelm Pauck and Francis Miller, *The Church Against the World*, was a clarion call for a reclaiming of the church's witness as distinct from the general culture. Niebuhr described the church as captive:

> The captive church ... seeks to prove its usefulness to civilization, in terms of civilization's own demands. It is a church which has lost the distinctive note and the earnestness of a Christian discipline of life and has become what every religious institution tends to become—the teacher of the prevailing code of morals and the pantheon of the social gods.[11]

Implicit in the argument was the assertion that the church was more than a voluntary association determined by sociological forces.

The normative assertion of what the church ought to be, expressed in *The Church Against the World*, no doubt contributed to Niebuhr's unhappiness with the reductionist tendency of *The Social Sources of Denominationalism*. It was not that the former analysis was incorrect, it was incomplete. The dynamic vitalizing element of the church's life was its faith, its immediate relationship to the transcendent Lord of all creation, the Sovereign God himself. This aspect of the church was not adequately accounted for in a sociological analysis. The reasons the church manifested itself in certain ways could be explained, but the explanation did not account for the existence of the Christian faith which produced the church. Most significantly, while the sociological analysis "could deal with the religion which was dependent on culture it left unexplained the faith which is *independent*, which is aggressive rather than passive, and which *molds culture* instead of being molded by it."[12]

Niebuhr might have written that the sociological analysis failed to account for the unique authority of Christian faith, distinct from worldly authority, in those times when faith became truly vital. *The Kingdom of God in America* demonstrated the way in which a significantly different understanding of the church emerged from a study which took the claims of transcendent reality and providential faith, on the part of the central figures of church history, as real and significant. Going to the sources produced by the great American religious leaders, Niebuhr found that underlying their formative theological positions was a shared perception of God's sovereignty and a conviction that the key to constructive theological work lay primarily in the immediate vitalizing presence of God. This vitalizing presence determined the character of Christianity and made it dynamic rather than static. The reality of Christianity could be understood, therefore, only if it were perceived as a movement rather than as an institution or multiple institutions.[13]

Because true Christianity was movement, it was perverted if it suffered rigidification of doctrine, creed, or ethical position, or if it became too intent on narrow focus and the importance of particularity. To guard against becoming static and allowing encrustations to assume central importance—or even to be used as tests of faith—Christian community needed ever to recognize the dynamic presence of God, which relativized all limited perspective and, if rightly perceived, kept the church in movement. Niebuhr's study of the American church convinced him that the high points of religious renewal came when men's spirits, minds, and bodies were awakened to the immediate reality of God. When God's immediate presence was most real, the Christian movement received a vision of God's sovereignty, and sensed a meaning in all of life, which shattered the comfortable institutionalization which plagued it.[14]

The concerns of *The Kingdom of God in America* brought Niebuhr into congenial relationship with the thought of Jonathan Edwards and Horace Bushnell.[15] Their emphasis on the believer's relationship with God and the authority of the sense of the heart, which alone was able to revitalize a captive church, was essential if the church were to disengage itself from the stranglehold the world held on it in the twenties and early thirties and to reclaim its distinctive message. Recovery of theology in America would be dependent on asserting once again the unique and utter sovereignty of God and the centrality of the Christian community as a context for theological reflection. Only so was the individual self placed in perspective and authority for Christianity distinguished both from the self and from the world.

3

THE PRIMACY OF REVELATION

The crisis of authority in American theology during the first three decades of the twentieth century was in part attributable to awareness on the part of Christian thinkers that historical criticism and sophisticated methods of comparative cultural studies were relativizing claims once taken for granted. The historical situation occupied by a person at any given time appeared to be determinative for his perception of any reality, including religious reality. The way in which claims were made for the reality of religious insight, then, became crucial. Niebuhr believed that the key to clarification with regard to Christian truth might be achieved through renewed attention to the concept of revelation.

In the years before historical criticism emerged, it was possible and plausible for a culture to understand its life-style, belief patterns, and convictions with regard to the ultimate meaning of life as normative. Individual deviation was regarded as misguided and sometimes as pathological. Nineteenth-century developments, already noted in this study, shattered such easy assumptions. No one culture could repose in the certainty of its normative significance. Gradual recognition of this development hastened the process sociologists refer to as secularization. World views which assumed divine sanction were studied by looking only at objectively observable phenomena without regard to their claims of truth. Niebuhr was greatly impressed and deeply interested in historical criticism and sociological methodology. He was unhappy, however, with the reductionist view which suggested that scientifically objective analysis was capable of doing justice to all reality. Could what was understood as scientific objectivity alone be authoritative?

In *The Meaning of Revelation*, Niebuhr proposed a nondefensive alternative to social-scientific positivism. Theologians who sought to justify Christian faith claims through appeal to scientific method, Niebuhr believed, failed to see the impossibility of such an effort; it was destined to futility because it did not account for the qualitatively distinct nature of the subject matter of faith. The answer was to be found in neither a wholesale incorporation nor rejection of scientific methodology but in an effort to understand legitimate distinctions among two primary ways of "knowing." Niebuhr endeavored to elaborate an epistemological theory which dealt with faith as different from the concrete phenomena perceivable by means of straightforward scientific research.

Niebuhr's argument was based on the conviction that there were two ways of "knowing" history. One of these was the external method which observed and interpreted the way in which institutions, societies, or movements appear to one who is not himself involved in the observed phenomenon. It was possible to offer rational and meaningful statements which could be shared and verified if such a method were used. Niebuhr did not discuss the complex issues involved in the evaluation of the external methodology. He recognized the problems of objectivity and was unimpressed with positivist assumptions. Nevertheless, Niebuhr credited the possibility of writing history, as it were, from "without." The Christian could thus do a history of Islam and adequately present the observable realities of the movement with accuracy, and such a history would be "true." Niebuhr would not grant, however, that this methodology of nonparticipant historiography was the only responsible way to do history. He determined to amplify the field of historical study, and thus go beyond Troeltsch's philosophy, by suggesting an alternative methodology which would be equally legitimate yet distinct and, perhaps, complementary.

The second way of doing history was as a self-conscious participant in the reality one sought to explicate. At one level, Niebuhr explained the distinction with reference to the contrast between a non-American interpretation of the founding of the United States and the account of the initial foundation recorded in President Lincoln's Gettysburg Address. On a more profound level, Niebuhr suggested that his distinction applied preeminently to faith. It was possible to explicate faith as a movement of historical significance and reality from without; thus might a sensitive Christian accurately write of Islam. It was, however, quite another matter to record "internal history." Participative engagement in a movement would result in significantly different understanding of the reality studied.

In this manner, Niebuhr accounted for the historical relativism Troeltsch had articulated, and yet opened the door for interpretation of the Christian faith as absolute—or, if you will, authoritative—for those who stand within. The concept of internal history allowed for a fundamental, qualitative distinction between interpretations of faith made from within the community and those, valuable but different, proffered from without. "There is a descriptive and there is a *normative* knowledge of history and neither type is reducible to the terms of the other."[16] Thus did Niebuhr create a basis upon which to build an understanding of authority. Internal history might provide authoritative norms for theory and practice even though external history, in comparative studies, observed radical relativism.

Having posited the reality of internal history, Niebuhr focused his discussion on the fact that the unique feature of internal history—indeed, that which made the distinction necessary—was the conviction shared by a community that one event was formative in its creation and perpetuation. This vitalizing and organizing principle, Niebuhr determined, was revelation. Revelation consisted in that part of inner history which illuminated all the rest of the community's existence and thus provided meaning both for the individual participant and the community as a whole. Revelation was authoritative because it ordered all extraneous parts of the total group experience and vitalized ongoing life.

For the Christian community, Niebuhr believed, the event called revelation is Jesus Christ. Revelation is not merely an event of past historical particularity, though it is that; it is continuing experience of the reality of Jesus Christ and the One Sovereign God to whom he points. Revelation is the perpetual relativizing of all finite claims; it is the in-breaking of the iconoclastic spirit which rejects all penultimate forms and articulations. Revelation revolutionizes men's religions and points them to faith:

> This conversion and permanent revolution of our human religion through Jesus Christ is what we mean by revelation. Whatever other men may say we can only confess, as men who live in history, that through our history a *compulsion* has been placed upon us and a *new beginning* offered us *which we cannot evade.*[17]

Revelation is authoritative; it is authoritative because its compulsion is to the heart rather than to the head. For this reason revelation creates internal history. Niebuhr's epistemological theory was that the truth of revelation is not gained through logic, through testing hypotheses, or through experimental analysis; the truth of revelation is personal knowledge; it is the sense of the heart. Niebuhr noted Pascal's comment that the heart, and not the head, finds its reason in revelation.[18] This is not to say that the reason of the heart necessarily conflicts with the reason of the head. It is, rather, to notice a difference in ways of "knowing." Niebuhr participated in an epistemological tradition shared not only by Pascal but also by Jonathan Edwards and Horace Bushnell, both of whom insisted that "personal knowledge," or the "sense of the heart," was essential for consciousness of God's vitality as well as for theological reflection.

Niebuhr's insistence on the nature of revelation as truth to the heart is the epistemological key to his treatment of authority. The sense of the heart was basic; it was the foundation upon which all else was built in Niebuhr's thinking. Theology was confessional rather than apologetic because the truth of revelation could never become real to one through the method of apologetics, through rational persuasion, or through philosophical argumentation. Revelation is authoritative in the fullest sense because it is self-authenticating. Revelation is not to be equated with Word, church, or any "knowledge"; it does not consist of "information"; rather it is a perspective, a reality of total involvement which reorients and directs life. Niebuhr used the words "intrinsic verity" to describe revelation; "we begin with it," he wrote, "not because it will lead to further knowledge but because it is itself the truth."[19]

Niebuhr's epistemology caused him to reject efforts to defend revelation against reason; such a dichotomy resulted in confusion rather than clarification because it was predicated on a false distinction which led to a misunderstanding of the task of theology. The proper work of theology was confessional proclamation. Niebuhr cited John Wesley, George Whitefield, and Jonathan Edwards as examples of Christian leaders who turned the church away from defensive attacks on reason toward its "proper work of preaching the gospel." The theologian's task was to explicate the meaning of the faith in terms of the faithful community, not to attempt a rearguard action against detractors.[20] Revelation needs no defense; it is authoritative but not authoritarian. Neither is it a once-for-all total package of information or prescription. It has to do, instead, with an invitation to life-style, to participation in a new realization of the created order. Thus is revelation a process in which men participate and grow. Those for whom it becomes authoritative must "begin the never-ending pilgrim's progress of the reasoning Christian heart."[21]

Richard Niebuhr held the anthropological conviction that to be a man is to crave meaning in existence. Man cannot live without some sense of an order which provides unity and cogency for individual life and corporate existence.[22] It is the nature of man to crave assurance that the exigencies of life are not merely random happenings; that, difficult as they are to understand, all things ultimately cohere. The authority of revelation is intrinsic because it is the provider of meaning; revelation is that happening which affirms coherence and order. The self confronted by revelation is inescapably drawn because it is in fact revelatory; "it makes the understanding of order and meaning in personal history possible."[23]

The themes of meaning and order are pervasive throughout Niebuhr's work and, as has been demonstrated throughout this study, are inescapably related to a strong conviction of God's sovereignty. God is the provider of meaning and order for creation; in him, according to Niebuhr, all things cohere. Revelation relates the self to the One God beyond all the many gods of men's lives; it relativizes all the lesser claims and points to the One in whom all things take on meaning. Such a God commands the loyalty of those for whom revelation has become real. The response of love and loyalty is inevitable; revelation is authoritative. "Love to God," Niebuhr wrote, "is conviction that there is faithfulness at the heart of things: unity, reason, form and meaning in the plurality of being."[24] The message of radical monotheism is precisely the affirmation that there is One in whom all things cohere, who is ultimately in control, and who provides meaning for all life. Nothing, whether natural calamity or personal tragedy, occurs which is not part of a total faithfulness in all creation attributable to the will of the One. It is often the case, of course, that particular happenings and experiences may appear to man as either good or evil; but confidence in the reality of cosmic faithfulness diminishes the significance even of these terms. Everything is a part of the whole, and as such is ordered and meaningful, even if in the moment this does not appear to be the case.[25]

It is the authority of revelation which compels conviction that all of life is ordered and that the order is meaningful. For this reason, revelation is primary for constructive theology and ethical theory and action. Niebuhr's insistence on the inseparable nature of theology and ethics was based on his anthropological and epistemological convictions, which related fundamentally to his thinking about revelation. Revelation is the primal force which vitalizes and organizes all life and results in active response on the part of men: "So with revelation we must begin to rethink all ideas about deity. We cannot help ourselves. We must make a new beginning in our thought as in our action. Revelation is the beginning of a revolution in our power thinking and our power politics."[26]

Niebuhr's affirmation of the authority of revelation does not solve the practical question: In what way are judgments to be made and shared? The nonindividualistic nature of Niebuhr's understanding of revelation is clear, but the practical implications require further artic- ulation. The authority of revelation becomes practically manifest in multiple ways within the faithful community. It may be well, how- ever, before examining the practical manifestations of the authority of revelation to summarize the essential ingredients of Niebuhr's treatment of the concept.

Revelation is primary because it initiates and perpetuates the Christian community; it is authoritative because it is irresistible and intrinsically true. Revelation is realized *within* community but it is not *of* the community; that is, the truth of revelation is existential but appropriable in the context of the faithful community. Revelation provides coherence for men's lives; it is the key to meaning and order. Revelation is variously manifested, it is not to be grasped, and it is perpetually new. It is the revitalization of every subsequent manifestation of faith.

4

MULTIPLE NORMS OF FAITH

This study has already demonstrated, with particular reference to Jonathan Edwards, that radical affirmation of the primacy of revelation intensifies the problem of authority. In varieties of religious experience, varied and conflicting theological norms and ethical directives are perceived; either anarchy prevails or some means of dealing with authenticity and community must be achieved. Richard Niebuhr, while emphasizing the epistemological primacy of revelation and insisting upon the existential nature of faith, interpreted revelation in such a way that he was able to deal with authenticity and authority. His answer is not unlike that proposed by Horace Bushnell. Knowledge of God is personal and existential; it is graciously provided and ultimately known through the sense of the heart. Still, it is not individualistic; that is, by its very nature, Christianity is tied to faithful community and can be expressed adequately only through multiple norms. Authority, therefore, cannot easily be isolated or identified, because it partakes of complex relationships among various indicators of authenticity. For this reason, Niebuhr did not set out in any one place to explicate authority; nevertheless, several clear principles with regard to authority may be readily distinguished in Niebuhr's writings.

The first principle has to do with the relationship between authority and Christian community. While faith is a function of personal knowledge, it is not appropriated apart from community. At the base of all of Niebuhr's thinking was the inescapable reality that the self is a self only in, and because of, community. The faithful community stands over against every faithful individual, not in the sense of authoritarian direction or control but as educator, guide, and context for growth and development. The community is the setting in which personal knowledge is gained; in turn, personal knowledge vitalizes and perpetuates community. Niebuhr explicates the seemingly paradoxical reality in a striking passage of immense importance:

> Without *direct confrontation* there is no *truth for me* in all such testimony; but without companions, collaborators, teachers, *corroborating witnesses, I am at the mercy of my imaginations.* This is true of the most trivial instances of knowledge.... If after the long dialogue with Mark, Matthew, John, and Paul, and Harnack, Schweitzer, Bultmann, and Dodd, I come to the conclusion that whatever Christ means to others and requires of others this is what he means to me and requires of me, I am in a wholly different position from the one in which I should be—if that were a possible position—were I confronted by him alone. *The Christ who speaks to me without authorities and witnesses is not an actual Christ;* he is no Jesus Christ of history. He may be nothing more than the projection

of my wish or my compulsion; as, on the other hand, the Christ about whom I hear only through witnesses and never meet in my personal history is never Christ for me. We must make our individual decisions in our existential situation; but we do not make them individualistically in confrontation by a solitary Christ as solitary selves.[27]

Niebuhr insisted that the starting point for Christian faith and theology was the unique authority of revelation, but revelation was more than something directed to the individual; it was a complex function of the individual and the community. To talk of "individual authority" was meaningless; in no sense did authority inhere in the individual. For this reason, theology had its starting place in the community of faith and found its authority not simply in logical precision, historical accuracy, or immediate religious experience but in a juxtaposition of all these in the context of the church. Religious authority cannot be individual because the truth of the meaning of revelation is manifested in no one way but in multiple norms through which the community retains the tradition, passes it on, and provides guidelines as to the nature of authentic existence.

Revelation can never be wholly contained in scripture, creed, inner experience, or church teaching, but all these function authoritatively. No one of these is finally authoritative, and no one way of ascribing a hierarchy of importance among them is either legitimate or possible. The responsible Christian cannot avoid wrestling with the multiple norms of faith. Niebuhr did not mean to stifle creative personal engagement in revelation, but Christianity is inseparable from community, and communal norms cannot be ignored by the Christian. Rather than straitjackets, such norms are vehicles of release from the bondage of either individual whim or institutional rule; they bind one to the community of faith, which is ultimately freeing because it places all human experience, including the self, in a context of meaning. Niebuhr thus endeavored to couple the immediate reality of revelation, which is ever creative of awakened religious vitality, with the revelation of tradition, which provides enduring witness to the reality of unchanging truth.

Niebuhr's complex view of religious authority meant that there was no easy answer to which one might point for clarification. To affirm any mediator of authority as absolute was theologically unsound because it allowed a relative object or institution to take on too great a significance. The multiple norms of faith all point beyond themselves to the one sovereign God.

The way in which Niebuhr used the Bible serves to illustrate his understanding of multiple norms. The tendency of the liberal theologians to pick and choose within the scriptures for passages congenial to their presuppositions was not in keeping with Niebuhr's conviction that attention need be given to the whole range of the biblical witness. Neither was he satisfied, of course, with a literalistic biblicism which turned exclusively to the Bible for authoritative guidance. The scriptures would not serve as an infallible guide; they did not do the job that an infallible guide was intended to do. Too many diverse interpretations arose legitimately in the Bible. In *Christ and Culture* Niebuhr illustrated the way in which a variety of interpretations of Christ, all of them legitimate, emerge in the New Testament.[28] The Bible functioned, therefore, as what might be called an "educational authority."[29] The Christian could not overlook the Bible, but neither could he fail to recognize other authorities which complement the scriptures and provide analysis and interpretation. The Bible is a part of revelation; its language, thought patterns, teachings, stories, and perspectives are constitutive of Christian community. The Bible is not synonymous with revelation, however, and the Christian need beware of bibliolatry.

The church, as a community of tradition and interpretation in which and through which men and women come to faith, is also a fundamental authority. The authority of the church is just as real and just as elusive as that of the scriptures. No one Christian community rightfully may claim to be the *one* true church, for multiple aspects of the Christian community are variously combined. "The presence of the Christian church manifests itself, then, in no one single way but in a multitude of ways," Niebuhr wrote; "there are no ways in which an infallible judgement may be made that Christian church is present."[30] The authority of the church derives from God. Certainly one of the tests of the presence of the church is its confession that its existence is wholly dependent on God. The church has no other reason for being than the promotion of the love of God and neighbor.[31] The self in community is dependent upon other selves for its being; the church's authority is based on the fact that the individual of faith cannot exist apart from the church. But, of course, in no sense is the church's authority absolute; it is derivative and it is relational, existing among the multiple norms of faith.

A third example of mediate authority which might be given is Christian tradition contained in creed and teachings.[32] The multiple norms of faith, such as scriptures, inner experience, creed, tradition, and church, which function within Christian community, complement each other and provide checks and balances in the self's evaluation of the nature and the authenticity of Christian experience and directions, or guidance, for the moral life. James M. Gustafson's discussion of Niebuhr's understanding of authority for ethics is applicable to the entire task of theological construction: "To use a spacial language, authorities are related to each other horizontally as well as vertically: The church stands alongside of the Bible as an authority, but it also stands under the Bible. No simple diagram of authority in Christian morals can be drawn."[33]

No norm which functions within human context can satisfactorily articulate the full truth of revelation; mediate authorities point beyond themselves to the One beyond the many who is the object of faith. Multiple norms check and balance each other to avoid distortion so that focus can be directed always beyond them toward the One.

5

CHRISTIAN COMMUNITY AND THE TASK OF THEOLOGY

Although the greatest portion of his career was spent in the university, Richard Niebuhr's primary community of loyalty and identity was the church. A university divinity school always occupies a place of peculiar middle ground between the essential minimal values, usually in the form of the canons of academic excellence, shared by disparate members of a modern university and the more particular value commitments of the church. Niebuhr welcomed the certain ambiguities of the theologian in a secular university; he insisted, however, that to be a theologian was to find one's fundamental identity in the church. Theology, according to Niebuhr, could not be done apart from the community of faith because it was in the community that revelation was realized.

Niebuhr distinguished between theology, which was dependent upon, and grew out of, internal history, and history or phenomenology of religion, which might be done from outside the particular community being reflected upon. Theology was the intellectual work of thinking about internal history; it was not simply fanciful exercise of a creative individual mind. By virtue of its place within the Christian community, it was accountable to the multiple norms of faith: "Theology, then, must begin in Christian history and with Christian history because it has no other choice; in this sense it is forced to begin with revelation, meaning by that word simply historic faith."[34]

Furthermore, the theologian's community of work and criticism had to be the community of internal history because, at the level of meaning and truth, only the community of faith could understand and evaluate his work. For this reason, theology had to begin with revelation because no other point of initiation was possible; only the believer could think about God. Niebuhr effectively removed theology from the general cultural setting; or, to put it another way, theology was always confessional and the apologetic task was largely impossible.[35]

By placing theology within the context of revelation, Niebuhr delimited both the proper object of reflection and the methodology by which the task was to proceed. The object of theology was not man's feeling, his experience, or his inclination, but God himself, as manifested in relation to the individual man and the neighbor through the multiple norms of faith. No theology could wholly capture the truth of the object; for this reason theological methodology had to make use of, and understand itself as part of, historic revelation. Niebuhr's theological method sought to identify the major positions represented in any theological issue. Theological antitheses would be investigated and understood not as alternatives among which to choose but as elements of truth, or general limits encompassing a boundary within which the task of theology would take place.[36] The method did not lessen the responsible freedom of the theologian but provided an authoritative context for theology. One cannot help but notice the striking similarity to Bushnell's method of comprehensiveness, in which he sought to examine multiple positions within Christian faith.

Basic to Niebuhr's methodology was the conviction that different points in time required varying ways of understanding revelation. The danger was that a particular articulation would become a standard for segments of the faithful community. Such a standard tended to supplant the proper object of theology and rigidification would set in. Historically, groups of Christians, in both churches and sects, distorted the gospel by emphasizing particular insights and making them doctrinal absolutes. Niebuhr was ever concerned to indicate alternatives within revelation; the authority of revelation would allow no absolute mediate authority.

Consequently, the methodological principle of balance was central to Niebuhr. Because every theological claim was partial, perversion was inevitable if theology were not informed with a constant awareness of the need for balance. Legitimate norms became destructive if they were valued for themselves rather than for their ability to point beyond themselves. Thus Niebuhr wrote, "Denominationalism not the denominations; ecclesiasticism not the churches; Biblicism not the Bible; Christism not Jesus Christ; these represent the chief present perversions and confusions in church and theology."[37] In his unpublished Cole Lectures at Vanderbilt University, Niebuhr remarked on the importance of the methodology of balance:

But when we think of the principle of balance we think rather of that movement into the future which none of us can escape and which the church cannot escape. In the course of that movement we are forever subject, I have suggested, to the winds and tides of the movement which may carry us too far to the north or south, too far to the east or west, even though they are the winds and tides in theology itself.[38]

The truth of revelation could not be wholly contained in any systematic theology. The theologian's mandate was to guard against excess and to remain accountable to the multiple norms of faith.

Having examined the variety of ways in which authority functioned within the thought and action of the Christian life according to Richard Niebuhr, it is perhaps well to attempt to isolate several generalizations which undergird various specific applications of the theme throughout his works:

1.   The problem of authority was central for theology. The reality of this point was greatly emphasized by complex theories of historical relativism. Niebuhr documented through sophisticated criticism the way in which unexamined assumptions could function authoritatively for theology, as in the case of racism or the equation of sin and poverty. The theologian had to do more than individual creative musing; he was perpetually responsible to an authoritative context.

2.   Ultimate authority could in no sense be captured by man for his use, and no one mediate authority could be absolute. Ultimate authority was God alone; revelation, which pointed man to God and to a perception of meaning and order, was mediated through multiple authorities which functioned within the faithful community. The multiple authorities provided limits within which the faithful self acted. Niebuhr did not restrict the action of the transcendent reality of God but trusted that the multiple authorities themselves allowed for and required freedom. Men were required to acknowledge and deal with authority, but true authority freed the self for faith.

3.   Theological reflection and ethical decision had to take place within a context of authority. The context of authority was the

faithful community, the community of revelation, community of internal history.

Richard Niebuhr's work ably demonstrated the distinction between authority and authoritarianism. Authoritarian efforts at ethics or theology propose to assert positions of unqualified certainty in accord with scripture, tradition, or creedal affirmation. In opposing tendencies toward authoritarian answers, some theologians reject all external standards in favor of man's own conscience or reason. This tendency was greatly encouraged in the late nineteenth century by progress in historical criticism and refined techniques of study which made relativism, ironically, appear to be an absolute certainty. Niebuhr proposed a way of thinking, knowing, and doing which accounted for relativism but asserted the reality of the absolute nature of the faithful community loyal to its internal history. Authority was freeing because it provided meaning for all the curious anomalies of individual biography and corporate history.

CHAPTER V

AUTHORITY IN CONTEMPORARY THEOLOGY

1

FRUITS OF CONFUSION

Theology cannot be extricated from its culture; sometimes reflecting, sometimes challenging, sometimes utilizing its context, theology lives in perpetual dialogue with its environment. American theology of the past decade was written in a setting characterized by rapid change and turbulent emotions. The war in Vietnam, claims of minorities at home, women's liberation, student movements, and domestic political polarizations affected all of America's major social and economic institutions. Old sensibilities were being discarded and new styles of life and thought were taking shape. Hardly any aspect of American culture escaped unscathed. Government, universities, churches, and business corporations came under attack. Examination of conventional social teachings about family life and relationships between the races and sexes brought about shifts in value patterns and public role expectations. Advances in science and technology affected such diverse fields as music and war, medicine and communication media.

Theologians were unable and unwilling to be indifferent to the excitement of the sixties. Efforts to interpret Christianity in terms of social action emerged; sometimes these were coupled with secular theologies which tried to take the materialism, transiency, and autonomy of contemporary urban man with utmost seriousness.[1] Much recent theological work has accepted as normative the assumption that traditional theological authorities are unable to speak to modern man and therefore need to be set aside if theology is to have any relevance at all. Current efforts in theology are the fruits of the complex social and intellectual dislocation of the past decade; this study has suggested that it is in just such times that the question of authority for theology becomes especially crucial.

The intention of this chapter is to apply the critical questions which have emerged in the course of the historical study of the problem of authority for American theology to contemporary theological works. The positions chosen for examination are intended to represent what seem to be major options currently being set forth in serious American theology. There are many persons worthy of study, and any selection, of course, is subject to individual judgment. I have chosen Langdon Gilkey, John B. Cobb, Jr., Gordon D. Kaufman, and Frederick Herzog to be the primary figures examined because they are influential in their fields and intellectually rigorous thinkers. Moreover, like those included in the previous chapters, each understands himself as a theologian and seeks to do theology by taking his own setting seriously while never overlooking the tradition in which he stands.

2

ULTIMACY IN SECULAR EXPERIENCE

Among the most discerning commentators on the state of contemporary theology is Prof. Langdon Gilkey of the University of Chicago. In his book *Naming the Whirlwind: The Renewal of God-Language*, Gilkey perceptively examines the contemporary cultural setting in which the theologian must work. The dominant characteristic he finds to be secular existence. The secular view of reality typically includes four main elements, which Gilkey calls contingency, relativism, transience, and human autonomy.

Contingency refers to the perception that the world is "ultimately arbitrary" and not a product of reason, meaning, or order. Gilkey cites a passage by George Santayana to describe contingency: "Matter is the invisible wind which, sweeping *for no reason* over the field of essences, raises some of them into a cloud of dust: and that whirlwind we call existence."[2] Radical contingency, attributable in part to discoveries in the natural sciences, coupled with sophisticated historical criticism, has produced, according to Gilkey, a widespread conviction of relativism. The problem of historical relativism is, of course, not new; as this study has demonstrated, it dramatically raised the question of authority for William Adams Brown. Brown, and his colleagues, sought to answer the problem of relativism by attempting to appropriate the methodological principles of science, thus claiming to establish scientific authority for theology. Such efforts at seeking legitimation for an absolute reality, Gilkey believes, are doomed to failure in contemporary secular culture; secular man can conceive nothing to be absolute; "all is relative to all else and so essentially conditioned by its relevant environment."[3]

The lack of an absolute is tied to a sense of temporality. The modern mind believes that all will pass; for everything there is a season, but everything and every season will pass. "All is in time, and time being in all things, each has its appointed terminus."[4] The grim and hopeless nature of the first three elements of secular consciousness, Gilkey notes, means that one's hope, if there is to be any, must come from man alone.[5] The affirmation of man is crucial to the secular spirit because there is nothing else; man's present and future are determined solely by himself.

Gilkey seeks to demonstrate the way in which the elements of secular existence have permeated all aspects of modern life, including church, school, and government. Authority formerly ascribed to these institutions of the common life is radically undercut by secularity:

> The modern spirit, at least in the West, is dedicated to the proposition that any external social authority—whether of church, of state, of local community, or of family—will in the end only crush man's humanity if his own personal being does not participate fully and voluntarily in whatever help that authority represents and in whatever forms his life may take.[6]

Autonomous man picks and chooses among "a pluralism of possible authorities" and thus, Gilkey concludes, is "without any absolute authority except himself." Secular man, is, above all else, man alone; and in this sense, man "has truly come of age."[7]

Churchmen have not escaped secularism; as they go about their daily lives, they are as secular in spirit as other men. This means that traditional theological language is used only in the rarefied atmosphere of church services; in terms of actual life, such language simply has no meaning. Traditional theological claims of a transcendent, absolute, sovereign God, as creator of the universe ultimately ordered and meaningful, do not appear to be vindicated in secular experience. It is for this reason that the death-of-God theologies of the middle sixties struck resonant chords of response. Gilkey, however, rejects these radical theologies as untenable because they are self-contradictory. One cannot, he claims, affirm both radical autonomy in man and Jesus as Lord. Moreover, the idea of Jesus' Lordship makes no sense apart from a conception of the reality of God.[8]

Nevertheless, while Gilkey rejects the radical theologies, he accepts their analysis of the meaninglessness of traditional theological language, methodology, and epistemology. "Radical theology," he writes, "may be dead, but its protests and its affirmations set the *sole framework* for *relevant* theological discussion today."[9] The theologian cannot avoid the reality of contingency, relativism, temporality, and autonomy.

Having established the inescapable necessity of working within the context of radical secularity, Gilkey offers a constructive theology of his own. According to his criteria, he asserts at the outset that he can "make no 'nonsecular' assumptions."[10] There is no place to begin, therefore, other than with the everyday human experience of secular man. Upon examination of human experience, Gilkey finds that human beings sometimes encounter states of affection which do not easily fit into commonsense material life. Everyone, at some time or other, asks questions which cannot be dealt with in purely empirical terms. In the complexity of modern life, persons spend most of their time seeking the variety of material goods and associations to which society ascribes importance as symbols of success and security. There are times, however, when a sense of the purposelessness and temporality of life catches up with one, when anxiety becomes pervasive, and one fears that life is in vain. Sometimes, for even the most secular of persons, the question of life's meaning emerges. When we ask the question of life's ultimate meaning and cannot find the answer in the commonsense world, Gilkey writes, "we have reached the region of our limits, for we cannot *create* the meaning of our lives any more than we can create their security."[11]

Gilkey's argument is that although the eventual encounter with the sense of limit is integral to normal human life, the *secular understanding* of reality is unable to describe or symbolize this most fundamental of human experiences.[12] Gilkey concludes that, if rightly understood, this secular experience of ultimacy corresponds, in some sense, to what Christians have symbolized with the word "God": "To know our contingency as grounded beyond ourselves, and so to be serene in the face of this contingency, is to know, in life if not in reflection, he whom we Christians name 'God our Creator.' "[13]

The thrust of Gilkey's effort is not to establish the reality of God but to demonstrate that the recognition by secular man of the experience of limit, or ultimacy, is a "defense of the meaningfulness of the language game of religious discourse."[14] In order to do theology in a secular age, the theologian, Gilkey insists, must find a "common ground with secular experience" from which to begin; the sense of ultimacy provides such a common ground. From this point, the theologian can move to systematic theological reflection free from the charge that his words bear no resemblance to worldly reality.[15]

Even a brief account of Gilkey's position clearly indicates that he does not proceed with reference to traditional authorities. In his insightful treatment of contemporary culture, Gilkey establishes that, for the secular mood, modern man is himself authoritative. All social and intellectual authorities are subject to individual consent; imposition of external norm is understood to have the potential for robbing man of his full autonomy. Gilkey does not challenge the reality of secular experience; he accepts secularity as inevitable. For this reason, he maintains that theology, if it is to be relevant, must adjust itself to the secular mood. Secular experience thus becomes normative, or authoritative, for the contemporary task of theology. Every theological claim is judged according to its ability to evoke consensual agreement from autonomous "man come of age." The acceptance of the authority of secular experience does not, however, inevitably require either Gilkey's method or answer; the analysis of the secular which informs Gilkey's renewal of "God-language" is shared by other contemporary theologians, who produce significantly different constructive positions.

3

A CHRISTIAN NATURAL THEOLOGY

John B. Cobb, Jr., a Methodist theologian who teaches in the School of Theology at Claremont, concurs with Gilkey's judgment that the modern world's secular view of existence cannot be ignored if the theologian is to be intelligible to contemporary men and women. Cobb believes that an ever-growing number of persons are "profoundly estranged from that vision of the world that Christian faith had long made the basis of our cultural common sense."[16] This reality presents a fundamental dilemma for the theologian because theological construction has traditionally taken place within a context which has assumed a vision of the world as creation, thus presupposing purpose, meaning, and order.[17] A secular vision of the world undercuts this historic conception. "Christian theology," Cobb writes, "is not possible if the dominant modern vision of reality is accepted as context and norm."[18]

Cobb is convinced that Christian theology is possible only if the radical secular vision which denies the reality of a purposeful creation is challenged. The challenge cannot, however, propose to resurrect historical theological conceptions. No challenge to the modern vision can be effective if it appears merely to be an effort to recover the past. The challenge must come instead from a wholly new vision of the future. This does not mean that the starting point is neutral; all theological efforts must begin from a Christian vision of the nature of the world. Such a vision does not, however, involve beginning with specific Christian doctrines. Rather it means, in Cobb's words, "that one begins with what seems to him, quite apart from self-conscious acts of faith, most indisputably true."[19] Cobb's view is that reality is truly ordered, meaningful, and capable of being analyzed; moreover, he contends that if man can understand his own experience in such a manner, the *"vision* of the world as creation" may be sustained.[20]

The success of a new Christian natural theology, Cobb believes, will depend on its ability to make sense of natural experience. Dominant secular theories of action tend to emphasize the historical, psychological, or sociological antecedents of any particular action. Thus, when examined, actions may appear determined, even predictable, according to previous factors. Cobb maintains that the totality of human experiences and actions cannot be reduced to previous determinants. He cites, for instance, the "concern for truth" and the "disinterested concern for other persons" as two examples of human action which cannot be accounted for simply with reference to the past. These aspects of human experience, which involve "the fresh claim of newly recognized normative possibilities," Cobb refers to as "the call forward."[21]

To emphasize the common reality of "the call forward," Cobb appeals to a diverse group of writers, including such figures as Nikos Kazantzakis, John Dewey, Abraham Maslow, and Henry Nelson Wieman. Human experience for each of these observers includes potential for the desire, ability, and willingness to break with the past and forge a new future. Thus is human life more than the sum total of previously determined actions. Despite evidence to the contrary, writes Cobb, it appears that "a man *can* decide against his past habits and against social pressures, not simply as rebellion against them, but as responding to the claim of truth, of the neighbor, or some ideal possibility."[22] History, according to this view, is not the place to look to understand the nature of man or the world; both can better be understood as part of a process of movement into an untried, but promising, future.

The "call forward" seems to be so real that it is not only within man's spirit but also "a unitary actuality" apart from man, influencing the totality of natural life. Cobb can thus write of "a vision of something beyond ourselves and our past that calls us forward in each moment into a yet unsettled future, luring us with new and richer possibilities for our being."[23] The unique and powerful nature of the "call forward" suggests to Cobb that the use of the symbol "God" is warranted; "what calls us forward has the unity and actuality as well as the worthiness of worship and commitment."[24] Establishment of the legitimacy of the use of the word "God" is not a "proof" of the existence of God but an invitation to further consideration of "certain aspects of experience rather than others."[25] Thus, man's attention may be turned from the rigidities of the past to the ever-new possibilities of a truly open future.

Cobb makes it clear that the relativism of contemporary culture has been a major consideration in the development of his Christian natural theology. The authority of Christian claims has been undercut by historical and scientific criticism. For Christians, Cobb writes, "there is a profound need to believe that the vision to which we cling is warranted by something more than its fading existence"; if a decision is to be made about the validity of the Christian vision, somehow we must be able to "touch the bedrock of objective truth."[26] The position Cobb works toward is one which he claims is but true of universal existence and, moreover, is understandable, and justifiable, in terms of human reason. If persons are to choose among visions, the viability of the Christian vision depends on its ability to convince "at the level of conscious persuasion."[27]

The theological position Cobb sets forth is primarily dependent upon the metaphysical philosophy of Alfred North Whitehead and Whitehead's American interpreters, especially Charles Hartshorne. The appeal is to the natural order of the universe, and to human experience therein, not through appeal to historical specifics but through analysis of universal, recurrent, or widespread experience.[28] One's evaluation of Cobb's natural theology therefore depends upon one's evaluation of the *philosophical* argument.

The fundamental assumption of Cobb's theology is that modern human reason is authoritative for constructive theology. His rejection of the radical secular vision is not a rejection of contemporary human reason; he believes, indeed, that his natural theology is more reasonable than the secular view of the world. Reason will not permit the authority of scripture, revelation, or church teaching; and every theological move must be tested before the judgment bar of reason:

Does not Christianity as much as any position live or die according to the validity of its truth claims? Must not these truth claims, like all other truth claims, be judged at the court of reason? Does not every attempt to escape this court of last appeal depend on ideas of authority or revelation or intuition, which can function responsibly only when they in turn are rationally tested? Is it not exceedingly dangerous to claim that some decisions or some areas of life are or should be free from the control of reason? ... My own answer to all these questions is affirmative.[29]

Cobb argues that his new adaptation of Whitehead's philosophy provides fresh options in theology which can be acceptable to the modern consciousness. His argument seeks to be intellectually rigorous, logically tight, and eminently reasonable. All that is required is intellectual consent to a philosophical view of reality.[30]

John Cobb's theology is based upon the assumption that any reversal of the decline of faith in the modern world will be dependent on a credible explication of Christianity in terms meaningful to secular persons. The philosophy of Alfred North Whitehead, Cobb believes, is a vehicle through which Christian faith can be translated into terms acceptable to the authority of reason and, therefore, may allow secular persons to appropriate the Christian vision of the world. The nonhistorical character of Cobb's Christian natural theology, which results from his dependence on Whitehead, however, is regarded as a weakness by some thinkers, who insist that secular culture requires that it is precisely *historical* reality which must be taken with profound seriousness.

4

THE AUTHORITY OF HISTORY

Gordon Kaufman, an ordained Mennonite minister who teaches in the Harvard University Divinity School, contends that theology can be meaningful for man in contemporary culture if the theological effort is approached from what he calls a "historicist perspective." Kaufman suggests that theological discussion must proceed by exploring the meaning of actual historical events observable and describable in human terms. *Systematic Theology: A Historicist Perspective* is Kaufman's attempt to demonstrate the fundamentally historical character of revelation; it is one of the few important efforts at a complete systematic theology by an American theologian in the sixties.

Kaufman's work is informed by the conviction that knowledge of

God is not to be achieved through examination of natural phenomena or human experience. Rejecting natural theology and the attempt to move to theology by way of experience, Kaufman asserts that both avenues actually require a prior ontological assumption if the reality of God is to be recognized. For God to be known at all to human beings, Kaufman insists, he must reveal himself.

The assertion of the necessity and reality of revelation implies the question of the *nature* of God's revelation. This question involves the theologian in the problem of authority: How is true revelation to be recognized? Kaufman argues that there must be a way to evaluate the *authenticity* of revelation; he notes that "we will only be sifting the variety of opinion with no adequate means of discrimination, unless we can believe that at some point Reality has unveiled itself before us, providing us with a criterion."[31]

The criterion of God's revelation, according to Kaufman, is nothing other than the incarnation of God in the radically historical reality Jesus Christ. It is this criterion which has been sufficient to evoke response of recognition from men and women and to engender Christian community. The incarnation is an affirmation of the historical revelation of God which is available to human beings through the observation of events in the world. "The formal significance for Christian theology of the doctrine of the incarnation," Kaufman writes, "is that it specifies the locus in human existence where God's defining revelation and presence are found."[32] The locus of God's revelation is Jesus Christ, an actual historical being. God has chosen to work in man's own history and existence.[33]

Kaufman is not unaware of the secular critique of theological discourse and religious faith in contemporary culture. The argument that God's revelation is fully historical is intended to preserve revelation, which Kaufman believes to be essential for theology, and, at the same time, to avoid any challenge to the secular rejection of mythological language. God's revelation, Kaufman insists, is able to be observed and analyzed according to canons of historical verity. Systematic treatment of the elements of Christian theology proceeds, then, according to the process of historical investigation. This means that exposition of the meaning of Christian doctrines is always in terms of historical actuality.[34]

A conception of original sin, for instance, is retained because Kaufman can make sense of the concept by examining specific processes of human life in the world which can be understood best through a recognition of the continuing *inevitable* reality of distortion, corruption, and selfishness on the part of *every* individual and group. The contention is that nationalism, racism, murder, imperialism, and other individual and corporate sins cannot be avoided.[35] Persons, no matter how noble, inevitably are implicated. *No* person can avoid complicity in the historical evils of the world; in this sense, Kaufman concludes, "original sin is inherited by all—not biologically, as Augustine argued, but historically—and there is no possible way to avoid it."[36]

The translation of Christian affirmations, as with original sin, into categories of a history understood in a commonsense manner as observable events capable of being tested by secular human reason, is Kaufman's aim.[37] This systematic translation is intended to strip the historical faith of Christianity of myth and mystery and make it readily available to the secular consciousness which has at its disposal critical historical tools and sophisticated modes of reason. Kaufman's effort betrays his commitment to a positivist view of history and his assumption that modern human reason is an authoritative judge of historical adequacy. Two issues, in particular, which emerge out of Kaufman's conception of theology and history, deserve attention.

The first of these has to do with Kaufman's belief in *reason*. The conviction seems to be that modern persons have received an inheritance of sophisticated tools for scientific and historical analysis. These tools enable them to judge the adequacy and truth of propositions and events in terms of truth or error, fact or fancy. Moreover, scientific and historical insights have provided men and women with greater knowledge not only of the natural order but also about themselves, their needs and desires, their hopes and beliefs. These developments have produced an intellectual climate which places great faith in the ability of human reason to recognize truth when it is found. Reason has established canons of truth by which all aspects of modern social and intellectual life can be judged according to clear, logical argument understandable to any intelligent auditor.[38] Theology, Kaufman insists, as "one among men's intellectual activities," cannot escape the scrutiny of reason; "it must be able to justify what it does and how it does it before the bar of ordinary human reason."[39]

The second issue is closely related to the first because it deals with the criteria by which Kaufman judges history and in turn uses his notion of history as normative for theology.[40] Kaufman adopts a positivist view of history and thus assumes the existence of historical "facts" readily available for evaluation according to canons of reason by objective historians.[41] An example of Kaufman's *Systematic*

Theology will illustrate the way in which his positivist view of reason and history functions authoritatively for theological reflection.

Kaufman subjects each of the traditional Christian doctrines to examination in light of the criterion of historical meaningfulness. The resurrection is both dramatic and key. It is, of course, embarrassing to a radical historicist perspective. Emphasizing Paul's account of the resurrection in 1 Corinthians 15 rather than the accounts in the synoptic Gospels or John, Kaufman interprets the empty tomb stories and the postresurrection appearances of Jesus as "hallucinations."[42] His treatment of the resurrection is admirably clear and appropriate to his system. Kaufman dismisses the Gospel accounts because they do not measure up to his conception of "historical"; that is, they are "unreasonable": "No doubt the early Christians experienced 'appearances' or visions and auditions of Jesus; but these are adequately explicable historically in *psychological terms*, and there is *no need to resort to the extraordinary hypothesis accepted by the early church*."[43] This passage demonstrates the functional authority according to which Kaufman's theology is developed. Psychological explanation and the evaluation of positivist history as to what constitutes "fact" take precedence over scripture and church tradition.[44]

Kaufman, like Gilkey and Cobb, accepts secular culture as the normative context in which theology is to be written; this means that theological construction is tailored in such a way that secular sensibilities can understand Christian affirmations. The major assumption is that, if rightly interpreted, Christian faith can be meaningfully appropriated by the contemporary mind. The "historicist perspective," according to Kaufman, is a vehicle which can make sense of revelational theology in the modern world.

5

AUTHORITY AND LIBERATION THEOLOGY

The first three positions examined in this chapter are basically similar with regard to authority; thus, while Gilkey, Cobb, and Kaufman produce diverse theological positions, each assumes the secular character of the modern world to be normative and accepts the secular human perception of reality as determinative for theological reflections. A significantly different treatment of authority results from challenging the inevitability of a pervasive secularity. In recent years a movement of persons who are convinced that the major theme of the Christian faith is the action of God in the world to liberate oppressed peoples has arisen. The theology which has been written by these persons is different from the positions previously studied in that the preoccupation is not with justifying the Christian faith to the skeptical secular mind but with proclaiming the liberating potential of the faith for the oppressed. This point of view, in fact, regards secularism as one of the tools of oppression because it obscures the revolutionary nature of transcendent faith. The central theme of liberation becomes clearest as it is applied to specific situations.

In Europe, Jürgen Moltmann, professor of systematic theology at Tübingen University in Germany, has been working on a political theology of liberation. In *Theology of Hope*, Moltmann offered a theological reconsideration of the theme of hope in Christian thought.[45] The problem, he claimed, was that hope was always seen in the future, especially after the death of the individual Christian, or at the "end time" for the Christian community. The reality of hope, which the Christian affirms due to the fulfillment of the promise of Jesus Christ, has important implications for the present, however. In the event of the resurrection of Jesus Christ, history has been proleptically completed. Thus in his recent volumes *The Gospel of Liberation* and *The Crucified God*, Moltmann insists that the Christian message must be translated in political terms in order to offer hope in the midst of the chaos of the contemporary world. Hope, then, is for the "now" as well as for the "not yet."[46]

A second arena where the theme of liberation has been prominent recently is Latin America. The traditional feudal order of society in Latin America, the political regimes which are a mockery of government, and the involvement of U.S. financial interests have created a situation of extraordinary political and economic oppression for vast numbers of people. Remarkable writing has issued from the struggle to raise the consciousness of the oppressed so that they can see and understand their own situation. Practical theologians have sought to explore the meaning of Christianity for the situation. Rubem Alves, Gustavo Gutierrez, Juan Luis Segundo, and Paulo Freire are some among a group of vital activist thinkers who are arguing that the key message of the Christian gospel is freedom from oppression.[47]

In the United States, liberation theology is being done in a number of settings. One might identify especially black theology and feminist theology. Letty M. Russell, for instance, has proposed that the contemporary women's movement may gain theological understanding through the theme of liberation.[48] Russell seeks to do Christian liberation theology within a feminist perspective; thus the women's movement becomes a particular hermeneutical principle by which God's liberating work in the modern world can be comprehended.[49]

Shunning the most radical feminist proposals—for instance, she does not reject Jesus because he was male, nor does she posit a literal female god—Russell sees the liberation of women as one aspect of the larger theme of human liberation, the central message of the Christian faith.[50] Russell does not simply make female experience authoritative for theological thought and action; the norm is instead a conviction about the meaning of genuine humanness derived from the conception of political and economic as well as spiritual freedom. It is this norm which seems to be characteristic of liberation theology despite an otherwise wide diversity of positions. The argument is that this norm derives from the Christian faith; but, as has been demonstrated, it is valuable to determine with precision the exact nature of the operative authority for theology.

It is difficult to generalize about liberation theology; indeed, one of the basic claims of the movement is that all persons should be about the task of thinking theologically in their own situation. Liberation theology rejects the deductive method of theological thinking—which begins with revealed truths from which theological principles are deduced—and insists that the only place to begin is with a particular situation, from which one may then induce the nature of God's work. Theology becomes an active process of groups and individuals constantly combining *action* and *thought* in all conditions and situations and is by no means the special province of highly trained academic experts. Authority for theology derives from individual and group experience, and theology, thus liberated, becomes a "tool" in the battle for freedom.

Liberation theologians tend to think in the context of a worldwide movement. Rich, northern, western, and white nations have for many years dominated the once-vast resources of the world. The resultant injustice and oppression is the situation to which Christians are now called to address themselves in action toward change. The key is understanding the central theme of God's relationship with his people set forth in the scriptures as a series of events explicating the good news of freedom. The message of the Christian faith, then, is one of "good news for the now" as well as "good news for the future." The "good news for the now" means revolution; that is, the message for today is that God requires a new ordering of political and economic life in order that the injustices of the past and present will be overcome.

In keeping with the plan of this book, particular attention will be given to the work of one U.S. theologian whose work currently is focused in the area of liberation theology in an attempt to understand the authority by which he works. Duke University professor Frederick Herzog, an American whose roots are deep in the German Reformed tradition, has recently set forth a position which explicitly rejects the assumptions about secularity upon which Gilkey, Cobb, and Kaufman build their theologies.[51] Herzog's analysis is that the experience of the secular, and the overwhelming preoccupation with secular reality, is not so much a general cultural condition as it is the specific condition of white, middle-class, privileged persons who have sufficient leisure and intellectual training to worry about their individual selves.

Herzog ties the secular to the self's preoccupation with understanding its own condition. Philosophically this attitude is represented by Descartes' initial consideration of himself as a way into conceiving the world. The process required the leisure and peaceful solitude that Descartes, as a French gentleman, could afford. Applied to contemporary life, only those who know comfort and means can afford to engage in the kind of self-examination which historically has given rise to the secular. Herzog's attack on the secular, then, stems from his equation of the secular with the privileged class. Only the privileged have time to contemplate themselves; and in order to be leisured, the comfortable must oppress others. The modern middle-class self, Herzog claims, contributes in numerous overt and covert ways to the wretched condition of millions in America and around the world. The political and economic systems which support a standard of living which encourages secularism and individualism are seen to be in direct opposition to the message of the Christian gospel. Because he identifies the secular as the product of selfishness and oppression, Herzog rejects the secular as normative, in any sense, for theology.

The practical effect of the liberal adoption of the secular as normative is that all theological formulations are judged with reference to their acceptability to the eyes of privilege and individualism. Such theology is scandalous because it proposes to describe God not only in terms of human beings but also according to a secular view of persons, which is real and meaningful only to one segment of humankind. The problem, of course, is one of authority; Herzog maintains that theology must have an authority other than secular culture. His claim is that the Bible is, and must be, the authorizing source and norm for theological thought and action.

The Bible is *source* because it is only in scripture that men and women know of Jesus Christ the Liberator, the one who mediates God in Christian terms. Jesus' life and ministry alone are able to open new doors of understanding which will allow persons to put behind themselves their lofty notions of private status and privilege and realize that God's reality radically relativizes all human material pretense. One can know of Jesus, however, only through the words of the New Testament.[52] Aside from the gospel message there is nothing one can know of Jesus; and because Jesus is the revelation of God, knowledge of God is dependent upon the Bible. The Bible is uniquely the source of Christian understanding of God, humankind, and the world.

Because of its uniqueness as source, the Bible is the *norm* for faith and action. The fact that Christian teachings grate upon the secular life-style does not mean that Christian conceptions ought to be adjusted to harmonize them with secularity; it means that secular assumptions are wrong.[53] The task of theology is not set by the world but by the Word of the sovereign God.[54]

Though the task of theology is set by the scriptures, the biblical Word does not simply emerge from the ancient texts in a pure and undefiled manner. The work of the theologian is to seek to unite the "biblical matrix" and the "contemporary situation."[55] The method involves total immersion in the scriptures in order that they become so much a part of one that the contemporary situation is seen in terms of scriptural meaning. If this is done, Herzog contends, the Word for modern man is that Christianity involves becoming one with the oppressed. Theology in modern America must begin, therefore, with those whom Fanon called the "wretched of the earth" or, in Herzog's words, the *marginales*, persons who are marginal in the modern world.[56]

As a hermeneutical tool, or focus, consistent with the need to begin with the *marginales*, Herzog adopts the concept "blackness." He is in danger of being popularly misunderstood, because, for him, "blackness" is not a *racial* quality so much as it is the wholesale rejection of all that white, middle-class, selfish, private lives entail. "Blackness" for Herzog means an affirmation of corporate selfhood, a mutual concern for the up-building of the whole. To *be a black self* is to be a "compassionate self"; to *think black* is "to be able to think from the perspective of the underdog"; to *become black* is "to give up one's glamorous white self-image."[57] The rejection of the white self is liberation; it is the freeing of human beings for whole life; it is the new self-image Jesus brought to the lives he touched in his ministry of love and reconciliation; it is a life of concern for the poor and downtrodden, of total self-denial even unto a death died on a cross for others.

The liberal image of man is unable to picture man as anything but potentially good; for this reason, liberalism is unwilling to accept the radical critique of white society Herzog feels to be inherent in the scriptures: "The trouble with liberalism is that it looks at man as mainly a nice fellow. And as a consequence we never come to understand what phonies we are as secular men, hucksters and imposters, exploiting and manipulating one another."[58] Those best equipped to understand the gospel message are those who in modern America most nearly replicate the oppressed to whom Jesus' ministry was mainly directed. This means that the infirm, the handicapped, or the imprisoned, as well as black, Indians, and others of nonwhite, non-Western origin, who consistently have been beaten down, are most likely to be able to hear the gospel of liberation. Political theology is thus not concerned with ideological politics but uses the complex forces of political oppression, and the drive for liberation, as an analogy to the freeing power of Jesus Christ. For this reason, whites must be shocked into new recognition of God's reality; they must "become black" to understand the truth of Jesus' message.[59] This does not mean that, as in a theology of politics, the overcoming of physical and political oppression is the primary aim of Christianity; nor does it allow identification of Jesus "with any contemporary figure, group, or power."[60] Real liberation is spiritual liberation for all persons, that they may know "the difference between the perfect and the sinful, the absolute and the finite."[61]

It should be evident that there is a significant difference between the liberation theology of Herzog and black theology. Perhaps best stated by Prof. James Cone, of Union Theological Seminary in New York City, black theology makes the black experience authoritative for theology:

> The norm of Black Theology must take seriously two realities, actually two aspects of a single reality: the liberation of black people and the revelation of Jesus Christ. With these two realities before us, what then is the norm of Black Theology? The norm of all God-talk which seeks to be black-talk is the manifestation of Jesus as the Black Christ who provides the necessary soul for black liberation.[62]

Cone has clearly established the black experience as authoritative for theological reflection; in this methodology, theology is judged according to its usefulness in the struggle for black liberation. Herzog distinguishes himself from this kind of black theology—and the issue is authority.[63] For Herzog, the Bible must stand over against all partial claims, including those of black people as a group.

The direction and focus of Herzog's theology is significantly different from those examined earlier in this book. He does not worry about secular doubts; he does not concern himself with God's existence. God's reality is not interior to the private self where the secular person looks for him. Moreover, Herzog recognizes authority as crucial and insists upon the biblical Word as a "Christian court of appeal" intended to allow the theology of "white Christian America" to emerge from its present "morass of complete subjectivity and privacy." Authority is understood to be a key issue because false authority has allowed for the equation of Christianity with selfish, white existence. "The basic issue," Herzog writes, "is whether we whites want to bow before a 'rock that is higher than I' or go on endlessly dreaming our private religious dreams."[64]

CHAPTER VI

TOWARD A RECOVERY OF THEOLOGY IN AMERICA

1

CRITICAL ANALYSIS OF CONTEMPORARY THEOLOGY

Historical study of the problem of authority in American theology suggests that the question has been recurrent; it has surfaced whenever seminal work has been done, whenever great watersheds were realized. Crucial periods of religious development are characterized by shifts in the locus of authority. Jonathan Edwards, Horace Bushnell, William Adams Brown, and H. Richard Niebuhr each proposed changes in the understanding of religious authority intended to meet the needs of their time and to allow for theological reconstruction in periods of social and intellectual dislocation. Contemporary American society, characterized as it is by uncertainty, confusion, and rapid change, is by no means wholly unique in the American experience; this fact suggests that the problem of authority may well be the key issue for contemporary theology.

The last chapter attempted to analyze major options in current American theology with reference to the question of authority. Langdon Gilkey, John B. Cobb, Jr., and Gordon Kaufman, although they develop a variety of theological positions, each largely accepts "modern secular man" as authoritative for theology. Frederick Herzog, working out of the context of liberation theology, proposes a significantly different position in that he rejects the secular assumptions upon which the others base their theology and insists that only the Word of God, expressing the truth and meaning of the primal, originating events of Christian faith, is authoritative. Having identified the authority by which these men propose to write theology, it is now possible to examine critically each position.

Langdon Gilkey recognizes modern secular culture to be inevitable.

He suggests that if theology is to speak to modern consciousness at all it will have to be able to demonstrate the meaningfulness of God-language within human experience. Gilkey begins with human experience, asserting that he will make no nonsecular assumptions. Within secular life, Gilkey finds the experience of "limit," which he claims to be universal. Upon reflection, however, it appears that secular understanding of reality is *unable* to handle this "ultimate": "We shall challenge the secular understanding of secular existence not on theological or metaphysical grounds, but on its failure to provide symbolic forms capable of thematizing the actual character of its own life."[1] The failure of the secular stems from its lack of "symbolic forms" appropriate to the *"actual* character" of its life. Gilkey purports to know the *real* character of secular experience and that symbolic forms alone are capable of describing this real character.

The problem with Gilkey's argument is that, in order to win the hand, his trump card must be the *inability* of the secular understanding of reality to deal adequately with the experience of limit, or ultimacy. He thereby attempts to distinguish between secular *reality* and the secular *understanding* of reality, and the claim is that the true character of modern human experience is not exhausted by secular understanding.

The distinction proposed between secular reality and secular understanding presupposes a *prior* authority which illuminates the *possibility* of such a distinction. This must be so, because if secular experience were really authoritative, as Gilkey himself describes it, it would be impossible ever to recognize the experience of ultimacy, let alone the fact that the secular lacks symbolic forms capable of symbolizing ultimacy. Gilkey does not take the secular with as much seriousness as he claims. His prior conviction of the reality of religious experience, which can be recognized and described, determines the shape of the argument from the outset.

Therefore, if one grants that the secular, by definition, shuts out all other views of the world but its own, and accepts Gilkey's insistence that there be no nonsecular assumptions, his argument, upon close examination with reference to authority, seems to be untenable. Secular experience, in the end, does *not* function authoritatively, despite Gilkey's claims to the contrary. The argument is undercut because of the failure to admit clearly at the outset the authority by which the theological effort is actually to proceed. Authority for theology is a crucial issue in contemporary America precisely because Gilkey's description of the secular is correct: The secular is exclusive; it rules out claims other than its own. Gilkey attempts to accept the secular *and still* do theology. His effort suggests that the attempt to have it both ways may be doomed to failure. It may well be that, if the secular, as Gilkey analyzes it, is inviolate to fundamental challenge, theology *is* untenable for modern persons. Gilkey's apologetic theology attempts to use the secular to establish the meaningfulness of religious language, but the effort breaks down because his argument is designed from the beginning to destroy the only authority he claims. Radical adoption of the secular as authority seems to doom constructive theology.

While Gilkey attempts to use the secular for what is, in the end, a challenge to the secular, John Cobb's theology is an exercise in redefinition. Convinced that the modern world, enamored as it is with "scientific reason," will not "buy" traditional theological formulations, Cobb seeks to triumph by developing a definition of God which is acceptable to the authority of reason. The result is a philosophical redefinition of God supposedly free of the embarrassing attributes which traditionally have been ascribed to God and which are offensive to "modern sensibility" because they "represent God as a restrictive and repressive force over against man."[2]

Analysis of Cobb's work with reference to authority indicates that, while questioning all traditional Christian authorities, it never questions the authority of modern reason.[3] Admittedly, Cobb is not claiming that his natural theology is completely self-sufficient; he regards natural theology as only a part of the total theological task.[4] He is trying to indicate that theological construction can be independent of traditional authorities. Nevertheless, if his proposal is to be fully cogent, examination of the authority by which his natural theology proceeds ought to be as rigorous as that by which he determines other authorities to be inadequate. It is not; the option that "modern sensibility" might itself be wrong or inadequate as a standard is never posed. Where historical Christian claims grate on the contemporary world view, therefore, they are simply discarded as "weaknesses."[5] The authority by which Cobb asserts that human interest in "truth," or unqualified concern for one's fellows, has no base in one's past but is a function of the "pull of the future" is never examined. The validity of modern reason as an adequate judge of competing conceptions of reality is not argued; it is assumed.

The theological construction Cobb achieves is a philosophical tour de force. It does not carry with it authority other than its reasonableness as a philosophical argument, and it appears unlikely that such authority is adequate for substantial effort at constructive theology.

Gordon D. Kaufman, unlike Cobb, insists that history is the key to viable theology in the midst of secular culture. Kaufman under-stands history, however, to be composed of observable and describ-able events, the veracity of which is open to judgment by human reason. Like Cobb, Kaufman insists that theology, if it is to be meaningful, must be able to justify itself before the bar of reason. The problem with this view is that it accepts human reason as authoritative without critically examining precisely what this all-sufficient reason is. What, in short, if modern human reason is not as capable of dispassionate evaluation as Kaufman seems to suppose? What if history is elusive and not as readily opened to "objective" analysis? Kaufman's reference to "ordinary human canons of validity and significance" is packed with assumptions which are in no way obvious and without need of careful critical examination.[6] The affirmation of reason as authoritative can justify theological argument only to those who raise no questions about the meaning of objectiv-ity, or commonsense reason.

In the Preface to his *Systematic Theology*, Kaufman writes, "What is required of the critic who is dissatisfied with my presentation is that he attack my central contentions about the meaning of Christian faith and my claims about the appropriate criteria and procedures for doing theology."[7] The questions raised here with reference to author-ity suggest that it is precisely the *criteria* and *procedures* by which Kaufman does theology which need careful examination.

Kaufman's acceptance of the authority of positivist reason and history makes his systematic theology ultimately untenable because it is forced into what is an impossible effort to reconcile Christian revelation and radical secular assumptions about meaning and history. The result is a systematic theology which is a curious and unsatisfy-ing blend of traditional theological construction and efforts at histori-cist interpretation.[8] Kaufman wants to be radically historicist in order to avoid alienating modern human reason while at the same time maintaining the reality of God and his revelation. Analysis of Kaufman's important effort suggests that acquiescence in the author-ity of secular canons of validity may do irreparable damage to Christian theological reflection.

Although Frederick Herzog proposes a significantly different alter-native for theological authority, the question addressed to him is the same one put to Gilkey, Cobb, and Kaufman: Is the authority recognized by the theologian adhered to consistently throughout the argument? That is, does the theological argument hold together on its own grounds?

By claiming the Bible as source and norm, Herzog opens himself to the problems which confront all those who propose the Bible as uniquely authoritative. The history of biblical criticism makes evident the fact that the Bible does not speak univocally. Because the Christian scriptures are composed of numerous and conflicting historical and theological positions, they lend themselves to a variety of interpretations. This criticism is not based on the secular contention that the Bible cannot speak authoritatively in contemporary culture because of its outmoded language or conceptual inadequacies. Taken purely on its own terms, the Bible yields a variety of fruits according to the interpretive criteria used.

Herzog obviously is not blind to the need for interpretive criteria; what he does claim, however, is that his hermeneutic principle emerges from the scriptures and thus is sanctioned by biblical authority. Deep immersion in the Gospel of John indicates to Herzog that the most nearly adequate interpretive principle for modern America is the oppression associated with blackness. This is so because experience of man's condition in the world indicates that the *marginales* seem to embody the aspects and potential of those whom Jesus, in his earthly ministry, sought to liberate. Herzog judges his translation and interpretation of the Gospel of John according to the standard of the liberating reality of corporate selfhood.

Herzog's argument involves careful study of the scriptures and analysis of contemporary worldly experience, with each feeding the other in order that each may be meaningful. Out of the scriptures he claims to be able to identify the black corporate self as the norm for theological interpretation of the scriptures; at the same time, contemporary experience suggests that nonwhite, selfless existence is the hermeneutical principle for contemporary American society. Herzog may bring with him to the scriptures more than he is willing fully to admit: that is, political, sociological, and economic convictions, acquired from a variety of sources, perhaps even the church, decidedly inform his understanding of John's Gospel.[9] The problem, therefore, may not be in Herzog's *conclusions* but in his claim that somehow these conclusions emerge in these terms for modern society out of the biblical matrix *and therefore are uniquely authoritative.* The theological point of contention has to do with the question as to precisely what it means to assert the unique and absolute authority of the Bible.

To claim the Bible as sole norm inevitably involves an authoritative principle by which the Bible is to be interpreted. It is obvious that not all readers of John's Gospel will understand it as does Herzog. How, given Herzog's position, are disputes within the church regarding scriptural interpretation to be settled? The Bible alone, if it is the "Christian court of appeal," does not seem to be capable of handing down a clear-cut decision. It appears likely that any effort at ascribing unique authority to the Bible will, under examination, prove to be inadequate, even if secular criticisms are rejected, because corroborating norms are always required according to which the scriptures will be interpreted.

Unfortunately, most liberation theologians do not state the authority by which they work as clearly as Herzog does. The result is that particular forms of consciousness come to determine theological thinking. Thus, for instance, black theologian James Cone asserts that the black experience must be the benchmark for theology; or Mary Daly insists that "woman consciousness" is the proper criterion for both thought and action; or the distinguished Roman Catholic Archbishop Dom Helder Camara of Brazil, in a lecture at the University of Chicago in October of 1974, states that Christianity needs to do with Karl Marx today what Thomas in his day did with Aristotle. Liberation theology, like all theology, requires the critique of the Christian community. Unexamined assumptions need to be uncovered and operative norms need to be clearly understood. Partial claims, whether of middle-class whites, blacks, oppressed peoples, or women, must not be ignored.

It is now possible to compare the nature of theological authority dominant in contemporary American theology with the positions examined in the first four chapters of this study. In the attempt to understand the history of the problem of authority, two issues emerged with particular frequency. The first had to do with the *social location of theology*, the second with the *nature of authority* operative for the theologian.

2

THE SOCIAL LOCATION OF THEOLOGY

The social location of theology refers to the context in which theology is done, the reasons for which it is done, and the persons to whom it is directed. Jonathan Edwards and Horace Bushnell continually emphasized their relationship with the church. While Edwards' conception of religious authority confirmed the epistemological primacy of the "sense of the heart," the intention of his theology was to explore the complex issues of faith rather than to translate them in such a way that men and women in the world would easily be able to appropriate Christianity. If anything, as this study has observed, Edwards' beatific vision was remarkably unworldly. Edwards' intent was proclamation; his conception of authority turned men and women away from themselves toward the sovereign God of all creation.

Bushnell, too, was thoroughly grounded in the life of the church. His complex treatment of religious authority juxtaposed an epistemological position similar to Edwards' with the community of faith. Theology was always in relation to the church, even when the theologian, moved by inner experience, stood in judgment of, or in opposition to, the church. Bushnell recognized the importance of the multiple norms of Bible, tradition, and creeds. This was true also of William Adams Brown, who, although he never served a parish church, understood himself as a minister and, throughout his career of teaching in Union Seminary, wrote for the church. Brown's effort to achieve an authority acceptable to modern consciousness sought to combine the demands of scientific reason with the rest of the Protestant tradition. The context of Brown's "modern theology" was the Christian community.

H. Richard Niebuhr's concern with the Christian community grew out of his understanding of the nature of religious knowledge and his conviction that Christian revelation was inseparable from participation in the community of faith. Niebuhr, in company with Edwards and Bushnell, believed that God's immediate reality was made known to the individual Christian through the affections, or the "heart," rather than through mere intellectual processes of comprehension. The truth of Christian faith was not to be appropriated through argumentation or pure rational evaluation intended to evoke consensual agreement to propositions of belief.

Historical study of authority for theology suggests that there is an inseparable relationship between authority and the community of faith. Christian community is never set over against the "sense of the heart," though the institutional church may be. Christian faith can become real only for the individual, but it can become real only for the individual in the context of community where the shared experiences of past and present Christians amplify and correct one's own experience. It makes no sense to talk of a person of Christian faith apart from the community upon which he is dependent and to which he is accountable.

The relationship between authority and community may best be understood as reciprocally dynamic. Authority not only is found within community but also serves to constitute community. The faithful community, for instance, exists because it recognizes its existence to be authorized from beyond itself; in this sense, Christian community is never self-authenticating. At the same time, authority is not heteronomous but is internally creative; thus, authority is not characterized as either a finally determinative imposition or a precisely explicable criterion by which absolute judgments can be made. Authority is the cohesive dynamic which orders and sustains the life of community. Therefore, to understand authority one must investigate the elements which make a particular community what it is and which inform the understandings and actions of that community.

Christian community is unique in that it conceives of itself as recipient of authorization and sustenance from the God who is alone ultimately authoritative. But as this study has demonstrated, there has never been consensus on the exact way in which absolute authority is translated for theological reflection and ethical prescription. Christian theology, therefore, must attend to the diverse penultimate realities through which the authority of God is exercised in the world. These mediate norms of Bible, creeds, church tradition, inner experience, and reason are factors in the total dynamic which serves perpetually to create and renew the life of Christian community.

The dynamic and reciprocal nature of authority means that Christian community is authoritative, not in the sense that it is dictatorial but rather in that it is the one context for Christian growth and experience. It is, therefore, the proper context for theology. Theological reflection for Edwards, Bushnell, Brown, and Niebuhr was always done from within the church; the process of theological thinking was intended to serve the covenanted faithful; the locus of evaluation and interpretation was the Christian community. Such a stance means that theology is tied closely to proclamation as the church seeks to understand and to announce its reason for being.

At least three of the contemporary theologians examined in this study appear to provide a rather sharp contrast with the historical figures in regard to Christian community as the locus of authority. Langdon Gilkey and John Cobb seem clearly to be writing for secular consciousness rather than for the church. Instead of calling modern men and women into question in terms of the gospel, they have determined that the gospel must be called into question in terms of secular experience. Although, in the final analysis, Gilkey criticizes the secular understanding of reality, he claims to do so within the premises of the secular itself, asserting that the secular is authoritative and can be challenged only on its own grounds. Cobb is interested in transposing the Christian conception of reality into a philosophical system potentially acceptable to contemporary culture. The effort seems largely aimed at a select group of intellectuals for whom complex philosophical arguments may be meaningful. The assumption of both Gilkey and Cobb apparently is that if Christianity can be translated into acceptable modern language, and therefore be intellectually understood, it may become a viable option for the secular mind.

Kaufman's insistence on the revelational character of Christian faith necessitates a greater concern for the church than that evidenced in the theology of Gilkey or Cobb. Nevertheless, Kaufman's theology seems to be written not so much for the community of faith as for those who wish to judge Christianity according to a positivist view of history. The intention of Kaufman's theology is to make Christianity acceptable to men and women who believe in the ascendancy of human intellect and the ability of human reason to evaluate truth. Here is an epistemological position radically different from that espoused by Edwards, Bushnell, or Niebuhr. Kaufman seeks to demonstrate that Christianity can be interpreted so that it will in no way grate upon a commonsense, factual view of historical development.

Unlike Gilkey, Cobb, and Kaufman, Frederick Herzog does not assume the authority of the sophisticated intellectual; his work is a thorough critique of secular assumptions. It is difficult, however, to understand exactly what the social location of theology is for him. Although Herzog intends to base his theology in the church, he seems to reject the institutional church and to assert the presence of the church among the *marginales*.[10] The institutional church is criticized as white, self-serving, and secularized. Nevertheless, Herzog does not call for dissociation from the church but for an attempt to redirect it.[11] He writes:

> In order to become Christians we must begin with the church, the traditional, visible church where the reality of the liberation church at best breaks through only from afar like the rays of the rising sun. But here my pen breaks to pieces. Deep down inside I know that the liberation church has nothing visibly radiant about it. . . . Thus the life of the disciple becomes an "impossible" one. He knows he must work for something other than the ecclesiastical establishment, and yet he must begin his work within its bounds.[12]

The key to understanding the inner tension in Herzog's treatment of the church may be this affirmation: "If there is church of Jesus Christ it is a miracle."[13] According to Herzog, there is nothing women and men can do to create or even to identify the church; in the end, it is the gift of God—and it may not be recognized at all.

The implications for theology of Herzog's understanding of the church are difficult to determine. On the one hand, it appears that the church is, and must be, the social location of theology; on the other hand, the unclarity about exactly what or where the church is greatly hinders the potential positive role the church might play in testing or evaluating theology. The unique authority ascribed to the Word tends to make questions as to church authority for theology of secondary importance.

A recovery of theology in America will be dependent upon the recognition that the social location of theology is, and must be, the Christian community. In recent years, American theology increasingly has been separated from the ongoing life of the church. In part, this has been a function of the process of secularization and the effects of secularization on the theological disciplines. Especially during the 1960s, there arose a gap between the academic study of religion and the practical work of constructive theology. In a time when secular consciousness was prevalent in colleges and universities, teachers of religion attempted to justify themselves and their disciplines to their academic colleagues through zealous claims that the study of religion could be dispassionate and objective. The growth of departments of religion at institutions supported primarily by the state tended to divorce teachers, publicly at least, from the community of faith. Academic religionists thus were inclined increasingly to study religion phenomenologically or historically.

Serious questions were raised about traditional disciplinary curricula, which originally were adopted for the college from the seminary, in whose graduate programs most teachers of religion were trained. Sociology and psychology of religion, historical studies, phenomenology, and comparative studies grew rapidly.[14] The movement away from the traditional theological disciplines in college and university departments has been accompanied by subtle shifts in the graduate departments of religious studies in America to accommodate students who wish to prepare for teaching in secular collegiate departments of religion. This has meant the admission of graduate students directly from undergraduate programs, and the concomitant elimination of expectations that the Ph.D. in religion involves thorough grounding in the whole range of the theological disciplines acquired in the professional schools of divinity.[15] There is, of course, nothing inherently wrong with these developments; the study of religion purely as an academic discipline is in order and, perhaps, overdue. Moreover, it makes no sense to require all academic religionists to have professional training. The growing distinction between the academic study of religion and scholarly work in theology does, however, have implications for Christian theology which have not been widely recognized or fully faced.

Most of the important theological work done in America in recent decades has been done in the leading seminaries, whose faculties have trained not only students preparing for parish ministry but also those preparing for teaching. The gradual shifts in the academic study of religion have affected the work of professor-theologians who hold positions in the distinguished graduate programs. The dominant community for teachers of religion has tended to become the academic community rather than the community of faith. Contemporary theologians seem to take their primary clues from their university peers rather than their peers in the church. The result has been the preoccupation with secular consciousness which has brought about the dominance of apologetic theological efforts which try to demonstrate the possibility of being thoroughly secular and yet, in some sense, Christian.

Secular theologies purport to allow those whose training and personal relationships have involved church and seminary to avoid total professional separation from this complex and still live without embarrassment in the world of the secular university. Academic religion now embraces a good many men and women for whom a traditional commitment of faith is not a reality but who have residual emotional or pragmatic attachments to religion. This position has been articulated sensitively by William Hamilton in his essay "Thursday's Child." It is Hamilton's observation that many teachers of religion simply no longer count themselves among the faithful. Those who have been trained as theologians, especially, are trapped, carrying on a career about which they feel increasingly uneasy yet from which they cannot practically extricate themselves. Thus, suggests Hamilton, the theologian he describes "can get a reputation for being skilled and interested in a field that he has no interest in whatever."[16]

The effort to be thoroughly secular and yet Christian has produced a theology informed by the authority of secular human reason. All theological propositions are judged according to their ability to allow secular persons to remain autonomous and worldly; contemporary relevance and acceptability to the eyes of sophisticated culture become normative for theological construction. Significant theological work is difficult to sustain under such conditions. The protean character of contemporary life means that theology which takes its clue from dominant current thinking becomes extremely transient and, therefore, effete. Van Harvey describes this reality when he writes:

> Contemporary Protestant theology, particularly, flits from one new frontier to another in ever shortening spans of time. The "death-of-God" occurs in 1967 but is superseded by the "theology of hope" in 1968-69 which, in turn, will probably give way to "black theology" in the early seventies.[17]

Secular theologians have often taken the dominant thinking and popular emphases of contemporary society and tried to demonstrate that Christianity, when rightly interpreted and properly understood, really is congenial to the current best human hopes or aspirations. Secular consciousness can be seductive; it seeks to convince the Christian that the "heritage of the national community," or the "best values of western culture," or even the "highest universal human aspirations and values" are, in the end, essentially the same thing as Christianity. To this way of thinking, the specific theological claims of Christianity only "get in the way" of achieving a much broader perspective.

The view that authority for theology must be functional in promoting the best values of the current cultural scene is illustrated dramatically by a brief quotation from an essay entitled "Toward a Charter for a Southern Theology," by Prof. Samuel S. Hill, Jr.:

> A theological and ecclesiological position, rather than being self-justifying on the basis of appeal to authority, must prove itself historically functional. That is to say, what the church promotes as ultimate truth and prescribes as desirable behavior must result in the cultivation of the noble values of human civilization: the freedom of man's spirit; mutual love and respect; a peaceful society; the dignity of all; the establishment of beneficial institutions and traditions; the creative expression of man's faculties in thought, art, music, literature, drama.[18]

Hill contends that authority for theology must be judged acceptable not on its own grounds but on the grounds of secular culture. That is, the adequacy of a theological position must be demonstrated according to its utility in the promotion of a particular conception of human community. Hill does not explain, however, how it is to be decided which conception of human community is to be normative. The issue at stake, of course, is authority. By what authority is theology to be done? According to what criteria will judgments be made with respect to theological construction and ethical prescription? Secularization promotes the authority of human experience; the secular academic community champions human achievements and potential. Efforts at secular theology, along with all efforts at theology, need to be examined with reference to authority.

The problems inherent in much modern theology become clear when it is understood that the secular is exclusive. A thoroughgoing secular perspective rules out constructive theology, or else the secular makes no sense. Serious theological work, therefore, is dependent upon demonstration that secular claims are at least as relative and ephemeral as the religious claims secularity challenges. If it can be maintained that secularization is neither inevitable nor irreversible, a recovery of theology in America may be possible. Theological thinkers will need to ponder the questions which are being raised about the adequacy of interpreting modern culture as thoroughly secular. At least two approaches to a reconsideration of secularization can be detected.

Prof. Frederick Herzog, for instance, argues that secularization is not so much a general cultural condition as it is a phenomenon of the white middle class. Only those who know comfort and means can afford to engage in the kind of self-examination which historically has given rise to the secular.[19] Herzog's attack on the secular arises from his conviction that the gospel totally undermines preoccupation with individuality, self-aggrandizement, and the quest after material comforts which he understands to be the very hallmarks of secularization. Herzog contends that only if men understand the radical *difference* between Christianity and the secular can real understanding of the meaning of God's Word begin to come about. Theology, Herzog appears to believe, cannot begin without a rejection of the secular.

A different kind of questioning of the secular has come from Peter Berger, a sociologist who, in his important volumes *The Social Construction of Reality*[20] and *The Sacred Canopy*,[21] analyzed the meaning of secularization for religious belief and commitment. In these books, Berger expressed the conviction that continued secularization was inevitable and irreversible. He recognized the consequences of such a view for theology but was resolute in his insistence that theology, if it were to survive, would have to adjust itself to the demands of the secular.[22] In a later essay, however, Berger significantly qualifies his earlier view. He insists that it is time for the Christian community to assert its own understanding of reality and not simply accept "modern consciousness." Berger does not reject his earlier analysis, which sees a structure of consciousness in the modern West which is not informed by a religious world view. Nevertheless, he suggests, the uniqueness and potency of this consciousness has been exaggerated. The issue, Berger notes, is whether the secular consciousness of the West is, as he once claimed, "progressive and irreversible." Now he points to significant evidence of a renewed interest in things spiritual and suggests that it may be the case that his own earlier projections about an "indefinite continuation" of secularization were incorrect.[23]

Perhaps Berger's most important observation, however, has to do with the question of the authority of "modern consciousness." Questioning the adequacy of secular exclusivity also involves the possibility that modern secular consciousness simply may be wrong: "After all, whatever 'modern man' may in fact think, how can one be so sure that he is right? Could it not be that 'modern consciousness,' far from being the pinnacle of man's cognitive history, may rather be the result of an impoverishment in man's grasp of reality?"[24] Berger's analysis is significant because it demonstrates at least one sociologist's recognition that the secular view of reality is one among competing views claiming obedience and loyalty. It is one thing to present a variety of empirical evidence to test hypotheses and to suggest trends; it is another to accept such hypotheses as descriptions of reality which are capable of prescribing proper courses of action. Secular theologians have assumed that the secular description of reality is sufficient to prescribe norms for theological reflection. The result has been a decided tendency to separate theological disciplines from the life of the church.

Christian theological reflection requires attention to the norms of highest scholarship, but, in addition to these, theology is dependent upon the multiple norms of Bible, creeds, inner experience, reason, and church tradition within the locus of the community of faith. Authority for theology involves the self-conscious affirmation of the church and the complex dynamic of the multiple norms.

This is not to argue that Christian theology does not belong within the secular college or university. Theology benefits from interaction with the wide range of academic studies, and, indeed, no great university or collegiate institution is complete without theological studies. The university alone, however, cannot sustain creative theological work. Theology is dependent upon the nurturing influence of the community of faith.

Perhaps what is needed in our time is a serious reconsideration of the role of the theologian as Christian scholar. Careful study of the development of the Christian tradition reveals that tension has always existed between those Christian thinkers who emphasized the vocation of the scholar and those who placed greater stress on the noncognitive aspects of the faith. The great theologians such as Augustine, Aquinas, Luther, and Calvin exemplify the vocation of the Christian scholar. The contemporary American setting, however, for the reasons herein described, is a far more difficult arena in which to practice the vocation than, for instance, the University of Paris in the thirteenth century or the University of Wittenberg in the sixteenth. A recovery of theology in America will be dependent on a willingness on the part of serious theologians to take the risk of seeking to provide new models—appropriate to our own day—for the vocation of Christian scholar. This much seems clear: Theology will be done by men and women who are participant in the self-conscious community of faith and who, while they are committed to the ideals of highest scholarship and meticulous craftsmanship in their scholarly work, recognize their primary community of identification to be the church.

CHAPTER VII

AUTHORITY FOR THEOLOGY

1

THEOLOGY AND CHRISTIAN COMMUNITY

There is a fundamental relationship between authority and community, and for this reason the church is the primary social context in which Christian theological reflection takes place. Authorization for theology thus is provided, in part, by the community in which and for which it is written. The words "Christian community," rather than "church," might be used in order to avoid the popular confusion that "church" is to be equated totally with the "institutional" church. The social location of theology is not exclusively the "institutional" church. Still, recognizing the problems and inadequacies of the institutional churches, one would be hard-pressed to demonstrate that any other social institution more fully approximates the intention of Christian community. The theologian must almost inevitably, then, be in some sort of relationship to that institution which historically has sought consciously to strive toward realization of Christian community.

Christian community is present where men and women understand themselves to be gathered not merely of their own accord but in response to God's grace. Christian community is self-conscious in that it openly affirms its allegiance to Jesus Christ as Lord and its intention to live in response to him. There is a wide range of manifestations of Christian community, and no absolute signs exist by which faithful community can be identified. The diversity of forms of the church is itself witness to the impossibility of capturing completely in the world the ideal of Christian community and is therefore also an affirmation that men and women can only approximate God's intention for them.

There are, however, traditional signs of the church that provide strong indication that Christian community is intended. The administration of the sacraments, the preaching of the Word, and the understanding of individual and corporate lives as wholly accountable to God in Jesus Christ are chief among these signs. By pointing to the traditional signs of the church, I am arguing that self-conscious intention and public affirmation are evidence of the presence of the church and an inevitable part of Christian faith. Cyprian, the third-century bishop of Carthage, meant to suggest this approach when he wrote, "Whoever and whatsoever he may be, he is not a Christian who is not in the church of Christ." Christian faith propels one into relationship with the church because it is the only human institution which openly affirms its loyalty to God in Christ and thus recognizes that inherent in its faith is a self-critical principle by which it must always be judged. The church, though ordered and ordained by God, is a human institution which recognizes its partiality; it is a servant people pointing away from itself to the God who alone is ultimate.

The church is the place of initiation for theology because it is the locus of God's principal activity. Though God's presence and involvement in the world is not limited to the church, God, through his Spirit, called the church into being that it might be the identifiable and functional agency for assuring the continuity of revelation. Luther rightly observed, "There would be no Bible and no Sacraments without the Church and the *ministerium ecclesiasticum*." While important historic differences continue to distinguish the several communions within God's church, the cultural, social, political, and intellectual realities of the last quarter of the twentieth century will increasingly force upon Christians the recognition that, in the final analysis, they are one in spirit because they share a unique faith and common heritage in the church.

Theology is servant of the Christian community when it seeks to interpret the meaning of the faith and the role of the church in light of its cultural context. Church theologians are those men and women who are specially skilled in helping the church to understand its reasons for being and in raising questions about its present manifestation. There must be a close relationship between theology and the life of the church. It is for this reason that some of the current trends in theology are problematic. Systematic theology seems to be confused about its relationship to the church and is increasingly a product of the professionals of the secular academy rather than of men and women who regard themselves, in some sense, as thinkers of the church. As I have tried to demonstrate, the social location in which thinking takes place influences the product; for theology, the implications are profound. In virtually every area of serious inquiry modern professionalization has produced a mentality of expertise which has removed most disciplines from the purview of the general intelligent reader. Theology certainly participates in this situation; gone are the days when lay men and women read serious theology. Have laymen changed? I think not. Theology has become the province of the professional, the long-range implications of which we ought to ponder. By no means do I intend to suggest that there is no role for the professional theologian, but I am insisting that the role of professional theologian requires attention to a larger community than simply professional peers.

If it is true, as I have argued, that in seasons of social and intellectual dislocation the key problem for theology concerns authorization for its work, then renewal of theology will be dependent on a reconsideration of the normative assumptions upon which the theological task is built. Theology initiates in the context of the Christian community; the locus of faith, therefore, may be understood as providing a setting of authorization which is exclusive as well as inclusive.

2

NORMS FOR CONSTRUCTIVE THEOLOGY

The contemporary Christian community exists within a rapidly changing world in which advancing technology has bolstered a secular perception of reality and accelerated the tendency for human beings to believe that they can do anything they will to do. It is not surprising that the church finds itself in the dilemma of trying to understand in new ways what it is and ought to be. The church does not stand alone, certain of itself and its message amidst the confusion which characterizes every other community and institution.

Contemporary theology reflects the lack of clarity so evident in the church. Theological thought has remained neither aloof nor unaffected, and it would be absurd to think that it should. Never has theology been divorced from its historical setting; theological thought has both reflected and contributed to the formation of its culture. The intellectual and social dislocation I have described encourages the proliferation of contending positions as to the nature of the Christian message. There is implicit in this study, however, the assumption that it makes sense to speak of authority for theology; that is, at some point, consideration must be given to the norms by which theological thought is to be governed. It is not the case that any theological system can today be produced, or for that matter even contemplated, that would propose to organize Christianity and articulate it in a single grand *summa*. Let it be clear, moreover, that this observation does not apply only to so-called "liberal Protestantism." The Rev. Charles W. Keysor of Wilmore, Kentucky, a prominent spokesman for conservative evangelical Christians, has charged that a "condition of total confusion—of theological anarchy—exists" within the contemporary church. Mr. Keysor has called for the development of a theology which proclaims the "core truths" of the Christian faith, although he admits that "it is by no means certain that all evangelicals are clear on what constitutes this core of faith—the principles of theology for which we are willing to die if need be."[1] The study of intellectual history demonstrates why it is impossible to assert absolute theological principles. Such certainties are not to be achieved any more, if ever they were. Are the only alternatives, then, the anarchy Keysor describes or the absolute certainty he longs for? Or is it possible to admit and celebrate diversity while at the same time to expect Christian theological thought to demonstrate some norms of accountability?

Historical study of authority for theology indicates that the reciprocally dynamic nature of the relationship between authority and Christian community does in fact give rise to a rich complex of norms by which the church lives and in terms of which theological construction is undertaken. These have usually been Bible, creed, tradition, inner experience, and reason. The intertwined and functionally variable character of these authoritative elements means that no singular theological interpretation can ever be reached; it also means that the question of authority must be antecedent to any serious theological work.

Jonathan Edwards emphasized the authority of the inner experience of God, which he referred to as the "sense of the heart." In doing so, he boosted the authority of the individual believer by giving epistemological primacy to inner experience; but, as this study has demonstrated, Edwards made great use of Bible and church tradition as both sources and guides to Christian faith. Bushnell largely shared Edwards' epistemology but placed greater emphasis on the common life. He insisted that theology give careful attention to multiple norms; his theory of comprehensiveness required use of the variety of mediate authorities within the context of Christian community.

William Adams Brown was a significant contrast to Bushnell and Edwards. Concepts of authority shifted in the last half of the nineteenth century, and Brown made scientific reason authoritative in his effort to interpret Christianity for the modern mind. He never abandoned the context of the church or the idea of multiple norms, but the criterion of judgment was always man's reason. H. Richard Niebuhr's approach to authority challenged the rational emphasis of positions like Brown's. Niebuhr, like Bushnell, developed a theory of authority which gave primacy to the immediate vitalizing reality of God and which insisted that the theologian be ever aware that no one mediate authority could ever capture the essence of Christianity. He worried that a particular conception of faith would emphasize particular insights and make them doctrinal absolutes. Such absolutes would supplant the proper object of theology, and rigidification would set in. Niebuhr spoke of the necessity for the theologian to maintain a sense of "balance."

Edwards, Bushnell, Brown, and Niebuhr all wrote in periods when social and intellectual dislocation brought the issue of authority for theology to the forefront. Edwards and Bushnell believed that the vitality of Christian faith had been sapped by stereotyped systems. They sought a renewal of theology by emphasizing the dynamic of God's reality and by rejecting narrow conceptions of Christianity. Brown's attempt to reconcile the Protestant tradition with modern reason made reason authoritative and is representative of the continuous liberal movement which has informed American theology since the late nineteenth century. Niebuhr took historical criticism and relativism seriously and suggested an approach to theology which stressed the revelational character of faith. He insisted that authority for Christian theology could not be judged from a stance outside the faithful community.

The contemporary theologians who have been examined stand in marked contrast to these historical figures, with the possible exception of William Adams Brown, in regard to the nature of authority for theology. Gilkey, Cobb, and Kaufman emphasize the authority of human reason, while Herzog makes the Bible uniquely authoritative for theological thought. A recovery of theology in America will be dependent on the possibility that theological thinkers understand not only the centrality of the problem of authority for theology but also the centrality of the Christian community as context for theology in which the multiple norms of the faith are allowed to test and correct each other.

Although the individual theologian may ultimately emphasize one or another of the multiple norms of Christian faith, it is only as the norms are allowed to remain in active interdependence that the full range of theological authenticity may be realized. No one mediate norm and no one theological vision can be uniquely authoritative, but this does not mean that theology is simply the product of individual preference. Authorization for constructive Christian theology results precisely from genuine accountability to the complexity of faith as it is expressed in manifold partial witnesses. The ongoing life of the Christian community testifies to the reality and the importance of the multiple norms.

The Bible is best understood as a product of God's interaction with his people. The functional authority of these unique writings of the faithful community has always been recognized by subsequent generations of the church. It is possible to understand something of the historical process by which the scriptures came into being. The New Testament, for instance, was written by persons who were members of the young churches spread throughout the eastern Mediterranean world. Active preaching, worshiping, and sharing in the fellowship of the gospel considerably predated the composition of the New Testament. As the eyewitnesses of Jesus' earthly life and ministry began to die, and when it was realized that eschatological hopes were not soon to be fulfilled, Christians sought to organize their claims about Jesus into documents which could be shared for basic instruction and evangelical purposes. Paul's letters and the later pastoral epistles were written out of the practical experiences and needs of the early church. There were many writings produced, and the process of canonization was the result of the need, already recognized in the early second century, for the church to decide which of the early Christian writings would be recognized as benchmarks of the new faith.

It is the affirmation of the church that God's spirit was at work in the men who wrote the sacred scriptures, and yet the inclusion of works of great theological diversity attests to the fact that it was not the view of the early church that the whole truth of God in Jesus Christ could be contained without remainder on paper in the words of scripture. It is not possible to understand with precision the process of canonization. The books included in the New Testament were those which had already demonstrated their usefulness to the church, which gave evidence of apostolic connection, and which were original in their approach. For this reason it is right to speak theologically of the Bible as self-authorizing. The Bible is the sacred canon because it speaks with authenticity to a degree beyond comparison with other literature. Men and women have found in it the power to change life patterns and redirect attitudes. It has been a source of strength and comfort in time of need as well as a harsh judge and prophet.

So consistently has the Bible offered insights for theological reflection, personal devotion, and ethical prescription that some Christians have asserted the Bible to be the unique authority for thought and action. Many Christians insist that if it is admitted that the Bible is not singularly authoritative the door is opened for all manner of error. The problem with this absolute position is that it proposes an inadequate understanding of biblical authority. In the course of this study, it has become evident that the Bible cannot be uniquely authoritative because it does not speak univocally. The diversity of the biblical writings signals the impossibility of capturing completely the truth of Christian faith in words. The scriptural witness focuses attention away from itself to the centrality of Jesus Christ as Lord.

One who reads the Bible must bring judgment and insight to it in order to receive the biblical word. This judgment and insight derives from Christian experience, from church teachings, and from the reality of life in the world. The fact is that readers of the Bible do—and must—bring with them tools for interpretation which include particular perspectives. It is exactly for this reason that the nature of the Bible's authority must be clearly understood. Persons who think they are accepting the Bible as solely authoritative may in fact be operating with any number of unspoken norms which are determining their interpretation. The Bible is authoritative within the context of Christian community because it is a primary component of the nexus of Christian norms.

The creeds of the church are a second important norm for theological thought, and major theologians have often used creeds as the foundation for determining the outline of their writings. Historical evidence suggests that from the very earliest days of Christianity disciples have tried to encapsulate in brief summaries the most important elements of their faith. Creeds became necessary when Christianity grew to include large numbers of persons spread over a wide geographic area who did not share common experience. The initial purpose and function of creeds was to exclude those teachings or affirmations which the early church corporately determined to be wrong rather than to be exhaustive compendiums of belief. The effort was decisively to reject false teaching rather than to propose any one creed as inclusive of the totality of the truth of

Christianity. No one creed can ever capture the full meaning of the faith. It was for this reason that Horace Bushnell urged the use of numerous creeds.

Creeds are authoritative as products of the church. In them, pioneers and perfecters of the faith have struggled to articulate their shared experience. As such, creeds are exemplary of the dynamic nature of authority; that is, they receive their authority from the Christian community and in turn are authoritative for that community.

Church tradition is a step removed from the formal nature of creedal affirmation but also is an important functional authority for theology. I understand church tradition to include the wealth of liturgies, polities, confessional writings, ethical teachings, hymns, and characteristic uses of language which have proliferated in the course of the church's history. The point is not to ascribe authority to specific components of church tradition; it is rather to affirm that the conservative aspect of the life of the church demands the theologian's attention.

One of the characteristics of the church is that it conceives of itself as an institution which must conserve the richness of its variegated history. It is obvious that the church's drawing board is never clean; new ideas, proposals, forms, and orders must compete with established tradition. Subsequent generations of Christian faithful learn from the communion of saints and test contemporary understandings of individual and corporate Christian life against the richness of the past.

As I have interpreted it, tradition is a norm for Christian theology. The theologian is not slavishly to follow the dictates of the past; constructive theology requires taking the present seriously and recognizing that the message of the church must be directed to the present. The theologian's problem is to interpret the continuity and richness of Christianity in the face of social and intellectual change. Christian tradition is both source and norm for theology. Study of the development of Christian tradition demonstrates that underlying a genuine diversity of interpretation are a manageable number of major ideas which, due to their perpetual recurrence, make for a remarkable continuity. It is this continuity which must be accounted for in theology; and, I think, it is thus possible to speak of church tradition as authority for theology. Significant departures from tradition need to be explained in terms of the tradition.

The norm of *Christian experience*, or practical life in the faith, has always been contributive to theology. The theologian's own life story inevitably affects his or her theological position. Moreover, Christianity affirms that God's reality is made known immediately to the individual. Religious knowledge is personal knowledge; faith is related to the affections; the knowledge of God is tied to the "sense of the heart." Men and women are not brought to faith by mere argument, because religious knowledge is not to be gained through a series of rational steps leading to commitment. The truth of God in Christ is personal truth; Christian faith is the gift of God's grace. God's immediate vitalizing reality is known to the human heart. Inner experience is thus an indispensable factor in theological authorization. Vital theology is dependent upon personal communion with God in total life.

No modern approach to authority for theology can avoid the decisive impact made upon all intellectual activities by developments in scientific and historical criticism which have tended to emphasize the potential of human *reason*. Although Christian theology has usually placed a high premium on rationality, the traditional norms of faith have been radically relativized by sophisticated criticism. Contemporary women and men are able to use the tools of reason to make discriminating judgments among conflicting claims and competing interpretations of meaning and value. It is no longer possible merely to assert traditional or supernatural bases for any kind of authority. This does not mean, however, that scientific reason itself becomes uniquely authoritative. My objection to the positions of Brown, Gilkey, Cobb, and Kaufman is in part owing to their apparent uncritical acquiescence in the authority of modern reason. I have suggested that the precise meaning of an appeal to commonsense canons of objective reason is not self-evident. Complex philosophical and psychological arguments can be mounted which seriously question human ability to "be reasonable." My point is not to reject reason; it is to suggest that reason is *one* among the vitally important multiple norms of faith. The importance of reason for the theological effort requires the contemporary theologian to give careful attention to currents of thought and artistic expression which do not originate in the faithful community. Theology cannot be extricated from its culture; it may utilize and reflect its setting as well as challenge it. Reason is certainly not to be discarded, but neither is it to become uniquely authoritative.

Theology is one way of seeking to understand God, humanity, and the world. All theology is partial and groping; it is, as Bushnell described it, a process, never a finished product. As a human process, it is constantly in danger of partiality. For this reason, the theologian

113

must always seek to test individual constructions against other positions. This means that within the context of Christian community, Bible, creeds, church tradition, and reason must all function as guides to the reality of God. No easy answer can be given as to the way in which the multiple norms function within the context of Christian community. To attempt a schema or particular method by which answers to specific problems might be achieved would be to risk rigidification and thus sap the vitality of faith. Each of the multiple norms must be considered, each must be accounted for honestly in the theological effort, but no absolute answer can be given to the problem of priority. As the historical study of authority for theology makes clear, theology is rigidified by the ascription of unique authority to any one of the multiple norms.

Perhaps the most important objection to my insistence that authority for theology consists in attention to the multiple norms of faith within the context of Christian community is that the position still allows for great diversity with regard to matters of doctrine and ethics; that is, it has not really provided clear-cut norms, and thus, in the end, the problems of balancing the multiple norms falls to the theologian. My study has suggested that this appears to be the only responsible way of proceeding. God alone remains ultimately authoritative; authority for theology must be mediate and, therefore, partial. This means that no unity of theological vision will be forthcoming; but this, too, is as it must be because of the impossibility of ever capturing the full scope of Christianity in a systematic theology. Diversity of theological views is to be celebrated as representative of one of the truths of the gospel. The effort toward Christian comprehensiveness, or balance, is well served by the conviction, attributed to H. Richard Niebuhr by John Cobb, "that men are usually right in their basic affirmative convictions but often wrong in their negations."[2]

The complex nature of authority for theology makes it impossible to isolate any one central characteristic. Authority functions always in a relationship which juxtaposes the experience of the individual with the experience of the community; for this reason, authority is dynamic and contributive to the perpetual process toward theological clarification. Clarity requires that sharp distinction be drawn between "authority" and "authoritarian." Authoritarian attitudes and relationships do not allow room for growth and development, do not involve real interaction between the holder of power and those over whom power is held. Fundamental to the religious authority which has here been described is the idea of a mutual interaction which points beyond itself to the God who is alone ultimately authoritative. Perhaps the most important observation about authority for theology is that it can never be an end in itself but exists only to move beyond itself to God. Multiple norms affirm the "servant" character of theological authority; no one of them exists for itself, nor ought any one of them divert attention to itself rather than to the God toward whom all attention is rightly directed.

Lest it appear that my treatment of authority allows for such a wealth of diversity as to be no authority at all, let us consider the implications of my position for contemporary theology. Efforts to reconcile Christianity with secular experience or contemporary human reason are called into question because of their tendency to accept the unique authority of secular experience and reason. Religious knowledge can never be translated wholly into categories acceptable to secular reason. It would seem, therefore, that theological efforts had best recognize the impossibility of accepting the assumptions of the secular world in an effort to build upon them and gracefully introduce Christianity as a congenial way of interpreting reality. Attempts to demonstrate that it is possible to strip revelation of all nonempirical manifestations are, I think, seeking to accommodate the biases of our particular historical period. I have tried to demonstrate that authorization for theological claims cannot be found through the appropriation of patterns of verification contributive to other kinds of knowledge. By definition, theological work implies relationship to the ongoing community of faith within which the multiple norms herein considered are determinative.

My view also calls into question efforts which take authority with great seriousness but try to identify authority for theology too specifically, usually by placing exclusive emphasis on one of the traditional norms. The most common of these positions involves the claim that the Bible alone is authoritative. Often it is argued that the assertion of the Bible as the sole norm is the position of the great Protestant reformers; this claim, however, fails to take seriously the precritical nature of early Protestant biblical interpretation. Moreover, it fails to see the actual way in which, for instance, Calvin approached the Bible. Calvin freely used the multiple norms of faith as he turned to the scriptures. Modern facile claims of biblical authority do not attend to the actual manner in which Christian theology must in fact be written. Careful investigation of biblical interpretation demonstrates that, whether they are understood and articulated or not, a variety of social, political, and religious norms inform any explication of God's word for a particular time and setting.

I suggested, at the beginning of this book, that the test of the whole effort would be whether or not there is a payoff for contemporary Christian theology. The payoff, as I see it, has to do with a clearer perception of the nature and task of theology. One of the major problems which has confounded contemporary theology has been a lack of conviction as to its proper role. Theologians appear to be confused about what it is they ought to be doing, and for this reason there has been a great deal of attention to what is called the human condition and the latest intellectual fashions. This study suggests that important theological work is dependent on a conviction that efforts at intellectual clarification of the Christian faith are valuable and essential and that this clarification is in service to persons who understand themselves to be a part of Christian community or who take a serious interest in knowing something about Christianity. This study is a beginning point; it constitutes a claim that the warrant for theology consists in a right understanding of the nature and task of theology. The theologian does not begin *de novo*, but as one who belongs to a particular community with a long tradition.

Authority for theology involves the prescription of a context of mutual accountability and catholic vision. Such a position calls to accountability theologies which are products of individual consciousness and do not originate within Christian community, and it calls to greater comprehensiveness theologies based on singular mediate authorities. Much of the contemporary theology written in America is neither done within the life of the church nor sensitive to the necessity of recognizing, and being accountable to, the multiple norms of faith.

Renewal of theology in America will involve a vital understanding of the importance of authority for theology. This means that American theology will need to worry less about what secular culture thinks of theology and more about the meaning of the Christian gospel and its implications for contemporary culture. Theology must seek to communicate the Christian truth from a stance within the community of believers which has been visited by God's grace. Theology is not a set of formulas, but neither is it merely individual musings drawn from personal experience, or sociological, psychological, or philosophical analysis. Apart from the church and its shared experience of God's grace, theology becomes either mere intellectual exercise or the fruits of private notions of the individual theologian. The authority I have described emphasizes the role of Christian community as a community of *mutual support* and *mutual account-*

ability. Constructive theology thus draws on a wide range of sources, but the context and manner in which it is done provides its authorization.

NOTES

INTRODUCTION

1. It is this use of "authority" which informs Hannah Arendt's discussion in her essay "What Is Authority?" in *Between Past and Future: Eight Exercises in Political Thought* (New York: Viking Press, 1968), pp. 91-141. Arendt brings strong normative judgments to bear on contemporary culture which enable her to assert that "authority has vanished from the modern world" (p. 91). It will become clear that Arendt has narrowed her concept too much; it is perfectly possible, logical, and meaningful to inquire of her: By what *authority* do you declare that authority has vanished? Arendt's moral-ethical analyses indicate that she is not without an "authority" by which she judges political theory, for instance. The limitation of the word "authority" to legitimate government actually serves to confuse rather than clarify. See Robert A. Dahl, *After the Revolution? Authority in a Good Society* (New Haven, Conn.: Yale University Press, 1970).

2. Max Weber's discussion of authority actually gave primary attention to what has here been referred to as the first sense of the word "authority." He was interested in governmental and bureaucratic authority. He identified three ways in which such authority might be *legitimated*: namely, on rational, traditional, or charismatic grounds. By discussing *legitimation*, however, Weber dealt with what is described as the fourth way of using the word "authority." His description of charismatic authority, nevertheless, deserves to be recognized as a use of "authority" apart from the process of legitimation. It is logical, as will be demonstrated, to inquire as to what *authority* legitimates charismatic authority. See Weber's essay "The Sociology of Charismatic Authority" in H. H. Gerth and C. Wright Mills, eds., *From Max Weber: Essays in Sociology* (New York: Oxford University Press, 1946), pp. 245-52. See also "The Types of Authority and Imperative Co-ordination" in Max Weber, *The Theory of Social and Economic Organization*, trans. A. M. Henderson and Talcott Parsons (New York: Free Press of Glencoe, 1964), pp. 324-423; see especially p. 328.

3. Jesus of Nazareth, of course, is a notable example of this. See,

for example, Matthew 7:28-29 (RSV): "And when Jesus finished these sayings, the crowds were astonished at his teaching, for he taught them as one who had authority, and not as their scribes."

CHAPTER I: AUTHORITY AND THE SENSE OF THE HEART

1. Perry Miller, *The New England Mind: From Colony to Province* (Boston: Beacon Press, 1953), p. 252.

2. For detailed analysis see Edmund S. Morgan, *Visible Saints: The History of a Puritan Idea*, Cornell paperbacks (Ithaca, N. Y.: Cornell University Press, 1963), pp. 124-38; also Edwin Scott Gaustad, *The Great Awakening in New England* (New York: Harper & Brothers, 1957), pp. 11 ff.

3. H. Shelton Smith, Robert T. Handy, and Lefferts A. Loetscher, *American Christianity: An Historical Interpretation with Representative Documents*, vol. I, *1607-1820* (New York: Charles Scribner's Sons, 1960), p. 199.

4. The revocation of the Massachusetts Bay Company charter, which came on June 18, 1684, was perceived to be punishment for the failure to maintain the faith of the fathers. See Brooks Adams, *The Emancipation of Massachusetts* (Boston: Houghton Mifflin Co., 1899), pp. 212-15.

5. Smith et al., *American Christianity*, I, 329.

6. "The Testimony of the President, Professors, Tutors, and Hebrew Instructor of Harvard College in Cambridge Against the Reverend Mr. George Whitefield, and His Conduct," Boston, 1744; reprinted in ibid., pp. 330-35.

7. See quotations from Isaac Stiles's "A Prospect of the City of Jerusalem," in Leonard Woods Labaree, *Conservatism in Early American History* (Ithaca, N. Y.: Cornell University Press, 1959), p. 62. See also Alan Heimart, *Religion and the American Mind from the Great Awakening to the Revolution* (Cambridge, Mass.: Harvard University Press, 1966), p. 109.

8. Edmund S. Morgan, *The Gentle Puritan: A Life of Ezra Stiles, 1727-1795* (New Haven, Conn.: Yale University Press, 1962). Morgan demonstrates that Stiles, an Old Light orthodox clergyman, was nevertheless a child of the Enlightenment.

9. Sereno E. Dwight, ed., *The Works of President Edwards: With a Memoir of His Life* (10 vols.; New York: S. Converse, 1829-30). Vol. I. *Life of President Edwards*. (This edition, hereinafter referred to as *Works*, will be used except where otherwise indicated.) Also Alexander V. G. Allen, *Jonathan Edwards* (Boston: Houghton Mifflin

Co., 1889); Arthur Cushman McGiffert, Jr., *Jonathan Edwards* (New York: Harper & Brothers, 1932). The best recent biography is that by Ola Elizabeth Winslow, *Jonathan Edwards, 1703-1758* (New York: Macmillan, 1941). The standard intellectual biography is that by Perry Miller, *Jonathan Edwards* (New York: William Sloane Associates, 1949).

10. *Works*, IV, 22.

11. *Works*, III, 562.

12. Ibid., 587.

13. Ibid., 588.

14. *Works*, V, 15.

15. Jonathan Edwards, *Religious Affections*, ed. by John E. Smith (New Haven, Conn.: Yale University Press, 1959), p. 116. Where possible I have used the Yale edition of Edwards' *Works*, of which *Religious Affections* is vol. II.

16. Jonathan Edwards, *Thoughts on the Revival of Religion in New England, 1740* (New York: American Tract Society, 18–.

17. *Works*, I, 60.

18. Ibid., 65.

19. See Miller, *Jonathan Edwards*, pp. 106-7.

20. Smith, ed., *Religious Affections*, p. 120. (My emphasis.)

21. Ibid.

22. *Works*, III, 5-89. Edwards intended that this dissertation be read along with the treatise *On the Nature of True Virtue*. The two were published together after Edwards' death. Prefixed to the original publication was the following editor's comment: "The notions which some men entertain concerning God's end in creating the world, and concerning true virtue, in our late author's opinion, have a *natural tendency to corrupt Christianity*, and to destroy the gospel of our divine Redeemer. It was therefore, no doubt, in the exercise of a pious *concern* for the *honour and glory of God*, and a tender respect to the best interests of his fellowmen, that this devout and learned writer undertook the following work." *Works*, III, iv. (My emphasis.)

23. *Works*, III, 12.

24. Ibid., 13.

25. Ibid., 39.

26. Ibid., 83.

27. See the important discussion of this problem in *Works*, IV, 198 ff.

28. See, for instance, *Works*, IV, 202: "And thus the Spirit of God leads and guides the meek in his way, agreeable to his promises; *he enables them to understand the commands and counsels of his*

word, and rightly to apply them. . . . He graciously gives them eyes to see, and ears to hear, and hearts to understand." (My emphasis.)

29. Frederic I. Carpenter, "The Radicalism of Jonathan Edwards," *New England Quarterly*, IV (Oct. 1931), 644.

30. H. Richard Niebuhr takes note of this fact in *The Kingdom of God in America*, Harper Torchbooks (New York: Harper & Row, 1959), p. 123: "In some respects the men who had come under the sway of the kingdom of Christ seemed less interested in political liberty than their Puritan ancestors had been. Wesley was a Tory in politics; Jonathan Edwards seems scarcely to have been aware of the political problem."

31. *Works*, III, 165-436.

32. Ibid., 94.

33. Ibid., 103-4.

34. Douglas J. Elwood, *The Philosophical Theology of Jonathan Edwards* (New York: Columbia University Press, 1960), pp. 6-7.

35. Alan Heimert, *Religion and the American Mind from the Great Awakening to the Revolution* (Cambridge, Mass.: Harvard University Press, 1966), p. 104.

36. Note *Works*, III, 104.

37. Rufus Suter, "The Concept of Morality in the Philosophy of Jonathan Edwards," *Journal of Religion*, XIV (July 1934), 266-67.

38. Reinhold Niebuhr, though he comes at Edwards from a very different perspective, arrives at this same conclusion. See *Moral Man and Immoral Society: A Study in Ethics and Politics* (New York: Charles Scribner's Sons, 1960), pp. 66-67: "Even when the religious sense of the absolute expresses itself, not in the sublimation of the will, but in the subjection of the individual will to the divine will, and in the judgment upon the will from the divine perspective, it may still offer perils to the highest social and moral life, even though it will produce some choice fruits of morality. One interesting aspect of the religious yearning after the absolute is that, in the contrast between the divine and the human, all lesser contrasts between good and evil on the human and historic level are obscured. Sin finally becomes disobedience to God and nothing else. Only rebellion against God, and only the impertinence of self-will in the sight of God, are regarded as sinful. One may see this logic of religion very clearly in the thought of Jonathan Edwards."

39. Winslow, *Jonathan Edwards*, pp. 241-42.

40. Ibid., 235. The quotation is from *Religious Affections*.

CHAPTER II: AUTHORITY AND COMMON LIFE

1. Samuel Hopkins, *The System of Doctrines*, 2 vols. (Boston: Lincoln and Edmands, 1811); originally published in Boston, 1793.

2. Ibid., I, 254-61; see especially p. 260.

3. Joseph Bellamy, *The Works*, 2 vols. (New York: Stephen Dodge, 1812). See I, 237-47 and 314-26; II, 127-28, 427-88, and 467-70.

4. William Ellery Channing, in his famous Baltimore sermon of 1819, set forth the basic tenets of the new faith. "Unitarian Christianity," *The Works of William Ellery Channing* (Boston: G. G. Channing, 1849), III, 59-103.

5. An excellent brief account of the basic motivations and beliefs of Transcendentalism may be found in Theodore Parker, *Experience as a Minister* (Boston: Rufus Leighton, Jr., 1859).

6. The most concise statement of New Haven theology is found in Nathaniel W. Taylor, *Concio ad Clerum: A Sermon Delivered in the Chapel of Yale College, September 10, 1828* (New Haven, Conn.: H. Howe, 1828). For detailed study of Taylor, see Sidney E. Mead, *Nathaniel William Taylor, 1786-1858: A Connecticut Liberal* (Chicago: University of Chicago Press, 1942).

7. The basic facts of Bushnell's life, along with interpretive anecdotes and personal correspondence, are found in Mary Bushnell Cheney, *Life and Letters of Horace Bushnell* Centenary edition (New York: Charles Scribner's Sons, 1903). Theodore Munger depends on Mrs. Cheney for the outline of Bushnell's biography and adds his own comments on the writings in his *Horace Bushnell: Preacher and Theologian* (Boston: Houghton Mifflin Co., 1900).

8. Cheney, *Life and Letters*, p. 499. The quotation is from Bushnell's friend the Rev. J. H. Twichell: "I have often heard him say that he was more indebted to Coleridge than to any extra-Scriptural author."

9. Barbara Cross, in her book *Horace Bushnell: Minister to a Changing America* (Chicago: University of Chicago Press, 1958), argues that Bushnell chose his theology to fit the preferences of a people who were undergoing urbanization and industrialization, who were better educated and less open to forms of religion acceptable in rural areas. Certainly Bushnell sought to minister in his contemporary situation, but Cross's interpretation does not take account of Bushnell's engagement with the problem of authority. She suggests, by inference, that his authority was "what the people wanted." "Anxious to reach his hearers, anxious for success as he groped to

find his full message, he was conciliatory" (p. 45). This study, I trust, will demonstrate that Cross's analysis badly misunderstands the complexity of Bushnell's theology because it fails to understand his treatment of authority.

10. Horace Bushnell, *Christian Nurture* (New York: Charles Scribner, 1864), p. 187.

11. Ibid., 31.

12. Ibid., 188.

13. Ibid., 91.

14. Ibid., 31.

15. Ibid., 91.

16. See, for instance, his discussion in *God in Christ* (Hartford, Conn.: Brown and Parsons, 1849), pp. 305-10.

17. Notice the discussion in *Society and Religion: A Sermon for California* (Hartford, Conn.: L. E. Hunt, 1856), pp. 20-21.

18. Full explication of Bushnell's understanding of family, church, and state cannot be given here. Of primary interest to this study is the fact that Bushnell *qualifies the individual* with reference to community. God's immediate revelation is a function of personal knowledge in community. On the family, see *Christian Nurture*, pp. 77 and 316. On the church, see "God Organizing in the Church His Eternal Society," *Sermons on Living Subjects* (New York: Charles Scribner's Sons, 1910), pp. 285-307. On the state, see *Politics Under the Law of God* (Hartford, Conn.: Edwin Hunt, 1844), pp. 6 ff.

19. *Sermons on Living Subjects*, p. 114.

20. Ibid., 115.

21. *God in Christ*, p. 263.

22. *Sermons on Living Subjects*, p. 123.

23. *God in Christ*, p. 332.

24. Irving H. Bartlett, "Bushnell, Cousin, and Comprehensive Christianity," *Journal of Religion*, XXXVII (April 1957), 104.

25. *God in Christ*, p. 311.

26. Ibid., 303.

27. *Christ in Theology* (Hartford, Conn.: Brown and Parsons, 1851), p. 81.

28. Ibid., 80.

29. *God in Christ*, p. 72.

30. Ibid., 73.

31. *Christ in Theology*, p. 33.

32. Ibid., 82.

33. Parker, *Experience as a Minister*, p. 16.

34. Ibid., 77.

35. *Christ in Theology*, p. 82.

36. *God in Christ*, p. 150.

37. Ibid.

38. *God in Christ*, p. 93.

39. *Christ in Theology*, p. 67.

40. Ibid., 53.

41. *Christian Nurture*, p. 161. (My emphasis.)

42. *Christ in Theology*, p. 90.

43. Ibid., 91.

44. Horace Bushnell, *Nature and the Supernatural as Together Constituting the One System of God* (New York: Charles Scribner and Son, 1871), p. 86.

45. Ibid., 511.

46. Ibid., 505.

47. John Edmund Howell, "A Study of the Theological Method of Horace Bushnell and Its Application to His Cardinal Doctrines" (unpublished Ph.D. dissertation, Duke University, 1963), p. 221.

48. Munger, *Horace Bushnell: Preacher and Theologian*, p. 382.

49. Perhaps the most recent example is Martin Marty, *Righteous Empire* (New York: Dial Press, 1970), p. 87: "Bushnell blurred nature and supernature with a romanticist's finesse." A perceptive interpretation of Bushnell, however, was given by H. Richard Niebuhr in *Kingdom of God in America* (New York: Harper & Row, 1959), p. 193. Unquestionably the best extended secondary source dealing with Bushnell is that by Howell, "A Study of the Theological Method of Horace Bushnell and Its Application to His Cardinal Doctrines"; for careful documentation of the misinterpretations of Bushnell, see pp. 224-28. The best brief treatment of the whole scope of Bushnell's work is to be found in H. Shelton Smith, ed., *Horace Bushnell* (New York: Oxford University Press, 1965).

CHAPTER III: AUTHORITY AND SCIENTIFIC REASON

1. Robert Wiebe, *The Search for Order: 1877-1920* (New York: Hill & Wang, 1967), p. 37.

2. Bert J. Loewenberg, "Darwinism Comes to America, 1859-1900," *Mississippi Valley Historical Review*, XXVIII (1941), 361.

3. Andrew Carnegie, "Wealth," *North American Review*, CXLVIII (June 1889), 653-64.

4. The Rt. Rev. William Lawrence, "The Relation of Wealth to Morals," *World's Work*, I (Jan. 1901), 287.

5. For a representative sampling of the best writing by Social Gospel advocates and an excellent historical introduction, see Robert

T. Handy, ed., *The Social Gospel in America, 1870-1920* (New York: Oxford University Press, 1966).

6. Representatives of the three views discuss "The Task of Theology" in *The American Journal of Theology*, XIV (1910), 200-20. Protestant orthodoxy is represented by Warfield, the middle road by Brown, and the radical modernist school by Smith.

7. William Adams Brown, *A Teacher and His Times* (New York: Charles Scribner's Sons, 1940), p. 75.

8. Ibid., 84.

9. Julius Kaftan, "Authority as a Principle of Theology," *The American Journal of Theology*, IV (1900), 684.

10. Ibid., 688.

11. Ibid., 689.

12. Kaftan made little effort to distinguish among the several positions within Protestantism. His primary emphasis was on Luther and Calvin, but even here he did not make the fine distinctions necessary to understand their doctrines of the authority of the scriptures. Brown made the same mistake; his criticism was mainly directed, however, against American orthodoxy. For treatment of the reformers, see Robert Clyde Johnson, *Authority in Protestant Theology* (Philadelphia: Westminster Press, 1959), pp. 36-41 and 45-48, and Rupert E. Davies, *The Problem of Authority in the Continental Reformers* (London: Epworth Press, 1946), pp. 130 ff.

13. See William Adams Brown, *The Essence of Christianity* (New York: Charles Scribner's Sons, 1916), pp. 15-16.

14. Brown's indebtedness to William Newton Clarke should be noted. Brown's book is a recasting of Clarke's *Outline of Christian Theology* (New York: Charles Scribner's Sons, 1898). Brown found Clarke's book excellent for teaching purposes but noted that "it had limitations of which I had become increasingly conscious. For one thing, it included almost no historical material. For another, it omitted the Church altogether" (*A Teacher and His Times*, p. 109). Hardly correcting Clarke's omission, in *Christian Theology in Outline* (New York: Charles Scribner's Sons, 1906), hereinafter referred to as *Outline*, Brown gave only one brief chapter to the church in a volume of 423 pages; see pp. 57-70.

15. William Adams Brown, "The Task and Method of Systematic Theology," *The American Journal of Theology*, XIV (1910), 215. See also the important statements on permanence and change in *A Teacher and His Times*, pp. 369, 371-72; also Samuel McCrea Cavert and Henry Pitney Van Dusen, eds., *The Church Through Half a Century: Essays in Honor of William Adams Brown* (New York: Charles Scribner's Sons, 1936), p. 15.

16. *Outline*, p. 229. Note that Brown's position in this passage is the one Theodore Munger erroneously attributed to Horace Bushnell.

17. Ibid., 202.

18. Ibid., 340. (My emphasis.)

19. On original sin see ibid., 288 ff. Man's potential is explained in *Beliefs That Matter* (New York: Charles Scribner's Sons, 1928), pp. 28-37, hereinafter referred to as *Beliefs*.

20. Sin is cogently defined in *Modern Theology and the Preaching of the Gospel* (New York: Charles Scribner's Sons, 1914), pp. 148-49. On salvation, see the same volume, pp. 131 and 158, and especially *Outline*, p. 297.

21. *Beliefs*, p. 47. It should be noted that although Brown's position on conversion is similar to that of Horace Bushnell, the *reason* for the position is different. Just as Solomon Stoddard had recognized the Lord's Supper as a "converting ordinance" in a time when religious vitality had waned in New England, so Bushnell articulated the view that, as an institution ordained by God to nurture and order life, the Christian family "itself is a converting ordinance." For this reason, Bushnell recommended that "the child is to grow up a Christian, and never know himself as being otherwise." Bushnell opposed traditional notions of conversion because they were not as *theologically* significant as perpetual religious development within the Christian family. The Christian family functioned as a converting ordinance; it provided a context of community in which one might grow to recognize the reality of God's vitalizing presence. Brown opposed traditional conversion because it was *more difficult to explain* in terms of the *new science*. For a summary statement from Solomon Stoddard's *The Doctrine of Instituted Churches* (London, 1700), see H. Shelton Smith et al., *American Christianity* (New York: Charles Scribner's Sons, 1960), I, 220-24. See also Thomas Schafer's interpretation of Stoddard's position in "Solomon Stoddard and the Theology of the Revival," in Stuart C. Henry, ed., *A Miscellany of American Christianity: Essays in Honor of H. Shelton Smith* (Durham, N. C.: Duke University Press, 1963), pp. 328-61. For Bushnell's position, see his *Christian Nurture* (New York: Charles Scribner, 1864), p. 77 and p. 10.

22. Brown, "Is Our Protestantism Still Protestantism?" *The Harvard Theological Review*, I (1908), 30.

23. *Outline*, p. 220.

24. *Beliefs*, p. 219.

25. *Modern Theology*, p. 53.

26. *Outline*, p. 56.

27. *Beliefs*, p. 217. See also *Modern Theology*, p. 60: "As an actual means of bringing about agreement among Christians as to the essentials of faith and practice the older way of using the Bible has not been successful." P. T. Forsyth makes this same point. He wrote: "The Bible is like the United States, ... the richest ground in the world for every kind of 'crank.'" See P. T. Forsyth, *Positive Preaching and the Modern Mind* (Grand Rapids, Mich.: Eerdmans, 1964), p. 121. This book was Forsyth's Beecher Lectures given at Yale Divinity School in 1907. Brown's *Modern Theology and the Preaching of the Gospel* is composed of lectures given in 1911. There is no evidence that Brown was trying to answer Forsyth, though it is interesting that the two sets of lectures were conceived according to the same basic outline. Differing radically in outlook, they both emphasized the problem of authority.

28. *Pathways to Certainty* (New York: Charles Scribner's Sons, 1930), p. 104. Hereinafter referred to as *Pathways*.

29. *Outline*, p. 70.

30. The use of the term "authority" in this context is somewhat confusing, and, for consistency, one wishes he had chosen differently. The concept of authority being investigated in this study is more akin to what Brown, in *Pathways*, called "certainty" than to the secondary and external evidence he refers to as the "way of authority." The distinction is only confusing, not difficult. In *Pathways*, Brown used "authority" to refer essentially to Bible, church tradition, or hierarchy. My use of authority is what he called "certainty." I am doing no violence to his meaning when I translate "certainty" and "absolute" as "authority," according to my definition, and thus bring *Essence of Christianity* and *Pathways* into consistency with his entire corpus.

31. *Pathways*, pp. 65-80; see also *Outline*, pp. 126-27.

32. "The Old Theology and the New," *The Harvard Theological Review*, IV (1911), 18. It was this article, given first as an address, which caused representatives of the old theology to charge Brown with heresy in the General Assembly of the Presbyterian Church in 1913.

33. *Modern Theology*, p. 210. (My emphasis.)

34. "The Task and Method of Systematic Theology," *The American Journal of Theology*, XIV (1910), 211. Also *Pathways*, p. 83.

35. *Outline*, p. 52.

36. Ibid., 345. Also *Modern Theology*, pp. 189 ff. Henry Pitney Van Dusen once observed that liberal theologians typically define

Jesus as normative for theology: "How are we to tell which Biblical 'perspective' is authoritative for Christian Faith? Where lies the norm for the discrimination of truth from error, of the enduring from the transient, of authentic Christian Truth from its imperfect anticipations and its illegitimate elaborations? As we have repeatedly insisted, Liberal Theology locates the decisive norm at one place: the mind and especially the faith of Jesus" (*The Vindication of Liberal Theology* [New York: Charles Scribner's Sons, 1963], p. 115).

37. *Beliefs*, pp. 101 ff.

38. Ibid., 345; see also *Outline*, p. 344.

39. *Beliefs*, p. 106.

40. See *Is Christianity Practicable?* (New York: Charles Scribner's Sons, 1916), p. 69.

41. *Outline*, pp. 412-23.

42. Brown believed the kingdom of God could be realized on earth. The latest evidence of this from Brown's own hand is his autobiography, *A Teacher and His Times*; see pp. 367, 370, and 375.

43. *Is Christianity Practicable?*, p. 131.

44. Ibid., 141.

45. *Modern Theology*, p. 212.

CHAPTER IV: AUTHORITY AND REVELATION

1. It is important to understand that there were varieties of American religious liberalism. Kenneth Cauthen sorts these out in his helpful volume *The Impact of American Religious Liberalism* (New York: Harper & Row, 1962); see pp. 26-37. On reason, see pp. 16-18. See also Lloyd J. Averill, *American Theology in the Liberal Tradition* (Philadelphia: Westminster Press, 1967), pp. 83-94. "Liberals insisted on the legitimacy of applying the test of rational intelligibility to Biblical and doctrinal matters, as to every other phase of knowledge and experience" (p. 83).

2. Cauthen, *The Impact of American Religious Liberalism*, p. 34.

3. Robert T. Handy, *The American Religious Depression, 1925-1935* (Philadelphia: Fortress Press, 1968). Also Paul A. Carter, *The Decline and Revival of the Social Gospel: Social and Political Liberalism in American Protestant Churches, 1920-1940* (Ithaca, N. Y.: Cornell University Press, 1954), pp. 31-95.

4. Bruce Barton, *The Man Nobody Knows: A Discovery of the Real Jesus* (Indianapolis: Bobbs-Merrill, 1925).

5. Sidney E. Mead, *The Lively Experiment: The Shaping of Christianity in America* (New York: Harper & Row, 1963), p. 186.

6.   The word is John Bennett's in his article "After Liberalism What?" *The Christian Century*, L (Nov. 8, 1933), 1403-6: "The most important fact about contemporary American theology is the disintegration of liberalism" (p. 1403).

7.   Paul Carter, in his *Decline and Revival of the Social Gospel*, looked to the "ministerial generation of the 50's and 60's" to prove whether or not the central ideas of the systems which, for shorthand, may be identified as "neo-orthodoxy" "can be made to take root in American cultural soil" (p. 231). In his review of Carter's volume, Sidney Mead rightly takes him to task for this statement, writing that a critique of liberalism "is one of the most constant strains in American ideology as exemplified in practice" (*Church History*, XXVI [Dec. 1957], 399). Similarly, Sydney Ahlstrom, in his article "Continental Influence on American Christian Thought Since World War I," observes that "there are very durable *native* foundations for post-liberal thinking to rest on" (*Church History*, XXVII [Sept. 1958], 269).

8.   H. Richard Niebuhr, "Ernst Troeltsch's Philosophy of Religion" (unpublished Ph.D. dissertation, Yale University, 1924), p. 100.

9.   Ibid., 220.

10.   See Hans W. Frei, "Niebuhr's Theological Background," in Paul Ramsey, ed., *Faith and Ethics: The Theology of H. Richard Niebuhr*, Harper Torchbooks (New York: Harper & Brothers, 1957), pp. 56 and 64; also James M. Gustafson's introduction to Libertus Hoedemaker, *The Theology of H. Richard Niebuhr* (Philadelphia: Pilgrim Press, 1970), p. ix. In regard to a unifying theme of Richard Niebuhr's work, Gustafson writes: "A case could be made for Niebuhr's preoccupation with Troeltsch's *Fragestellung* from the time of his dissertation to the publication of *Radical Monotheism and Western Culture*."

11.   H. Richard Niebuhr, Wilhelm Pauck, and Francis P. Miller, *The Church Against the World* (Chicago: Willett Clark & Co., 1935), p. 139.

12.   H. Richard Niebuhr, *The Kingdom of God in America*, Harper Torchbooks (New York: Harper & Brothers, 1959), pp. ix-x. The book was first published in 1937.

13.   Ibid., xiii-xiv.

14.   Ibid. See his chapter "Institutionalization and Secularization of the Kingdom," pp. 164-98; especially pp. 168-74, p. 186, and p. 193.

15.   See, for instance, *The Kingdom of God in America*, p. 172:

"Yet it was Edwards rather than Franklin and the Great Awakening rather than the rational enlightenment which really broke the fetters of petrified Puritanism and restored dynamic to the Christian church." With reference to the nineteenth century, Niebuhr wrote, "There were mediators who shared the protest against static versions of divine sovereignty, salvation and Christian hope but sought nevertheless to retain the critical and dialectical elements in Puritanism. Of these Horace Bushnell was the greatest" (p. 193). See also *The Meaning of Revelation*, Macmillan Paperbacks (New York: Macmillan, 1960), p. 2, hereinafter referred to as *Revelation*; and the essay "The Center of Value" in *Radical Monotheism and Western Culture* (London: Faber and Faber, 1960), p. 105, footnote 1, hereinafter referred to as *Radical Monotheism*.

16. *Revelation*, p. 49. (My emphasis.)

17. Ibid., 139. (My emphasis.) See also *Radical Monotheism*, p. 42.

18. *Revelation*, p. 69. Pascal wrote, "C'est le coeur qui sent Dieu, et non la raison. Voila ce que c'est que la foi: Dieu sensible au coeur, non à räison" (no. 13, p. 11). ". . . cette foi est dans le coeur, et fait dire non 'Scio,' mais 'Credo' " (no. 58, p. 25). *Les Pensées de Pascal, disposées suivant l'ordre du cahier autographique*, ed. by Gustave Michaut (Fribourg: Librairie de l'Université, 1896).

19. *Revelation*, p. 102.

20. Ibid., 2.

21. Ibid., 100.

22. See, for instance, ibid., 56-57 and 59. "To be a self is to have a god; to have a god is to have history, that is, events connected in a meaningful pattern; to have one god is to have one history. God and the history of selves in community belong together in inseparable union."

23. Ibid., 80.

24. H. Richard Niebuhr, *The Purpose of the Church and Its Ministry: Reflections on the Aims of Theological Education* (New York: Harper & Brothers, 1956), p. 37.

25. *Radical Monotheism*, p. 47. See also H. Richard Niebuhr, *Christ and Culture*, Harper Torchbooks (New York: Harper & Brothers, 1956), p. 192.

26. *Revelation*, p. 136.

27. *Christ and Culture*, pp. 245-46. (My emphasis.)

28. See especially *Christ and Culture*, p. 19.

29. James M. Gustafson in the introduction to H. Richard Niebuhr, *The Responsible Self: An Essay in Christian Moral*

Philosophy (New York: Harper & Row, 1963), p. 23. Gustafson provides a clear, brief evaluation of Niebuhr's use of the Bible.

30. H. Richard Niebuhr, "The Norm of the Church," *Journal of Religious Thought*, IV (1946-47), 14.

31. See *The Purpose of the Church and Its Ministry*, chapter I, section IV, "The Purpose of the Church: The Increase of the Love of God and Neighbor," pp. 27-39.

32. See *Radical Monotheism*, pp. 83-86. Niebuhr recognizes the value of creed as long as it does not become rigidified and conceived of as singularly authoritative; in this section of *Radical Monotheism* he contrasts and compares religious creed with scientific creed.

33. James M. Gustafson, introduction to *The Responsible Self*, p. 22. See also Hoedemaker, *The Theology of H. Richard Niebuhr*, p. 132: "In 'total life' we find ourselves in a complex field of many authorities."

34. *Revelation*, p. 16.

35. Ibid., 30. Note the following passage: "A theology which undertakes the limited work of understanding and criticizing within Christian history the thought and action of the church is also a theology which is *dependent on the church for the constant test of its critical work*. Being in social history it *cannot be a personal* and private theology nor can it live in some nonchurchly sphere of political or cultural history; *its home is the church; its language is the language of the church;* and with the church it is directed toward the universal from which the church knows itself to derive its being and to which it points in all its faith and works" (*Revelation*, p. 15). (My emphasis.)

36. Daniel Day Williams discusses Niebuhr's theological method in "A Personal and Theological Memoir of H. Richard Niebuhr," *Christianity and Crisis*, XXIII (Nov. 25, 1963), 212.

37. *The Purpose of the Church and Its Ministry*, p. 46.

38. H. Richard Niebuhr, "Theological Frontiers" (1), "The Position of Theology Today," Cole Lectures at Vanderbilt University (taken from a typewritten copy in possession of Prof. James M. Gustafson).

CHAPTER V: AUTHORITY IN CONTEMPORARY THEOLOGY

1. An excellent survey of the theology of the period may be found in Langdon Gilkey's volume *Naming the Whirlwind: The Renewal of God-Language* (Indianapolis: Bobbs-Merrill, 1969), pp. 73-145; hereinafter referred to as *Whirlwind*. Many books might be mentioned. Worthy of particular notice are: Paul M. van Buren, *The*

Secular Meaning of the Gospel: Based on an Analysis of Its Language (New York: Macmillan, 1963); Harvey Cox, *The Secular City: Secularization and Urbanization in Theological Perspective* (New York: Macmillan, 1965); Thomas J. J. Altizer and William Hamilton, *Radical Theology and the Death of God* (Indianapolis: Bobbs-Merrill, 1966).

2.   George Santayana, *The Realm of Matter* (New York: Charles Scribner's Sons, 1930), p. 94, cited by Gilkey, *Whirlwind*, p. 43. (The emphasis is Gilkey's.)

3.   From *Naming the Whirlwind: The Renewal of God-Language*, p. 48, copyright © 1969 by Langdon Gilkey, reprinted by permission of the publisher, The Bobbs-Merrill Company, Inc.

4.   Ibid., 53. Gilkey elaborated the implications of the rejection of understanding the world as creation in his earlier volume, *Maker of Heaven and Earth: A Study of the Christian Doctrine of Creation* (Garden City, N.Y.: Doubleday, 1959).

5.   *Whirlwind*, p. 57: "Little if any confidence or courage comes [*sic*] to modern man from his wider, cosmic environment where, as we have seen, all is blind, relative, and transient. . . . Whatever hope and meaning he may have must come to him from himself."

6.   Ibid., 59.

7.   Ibid., 255.

8.   Ibid., 162-63 and 177-78.

9.   Ibid., 25. (My emphasis.)

10.   Ibid., 247.

11.   Ibid., 350.

12.   Gilkey cites Stephen Toulmin's conception of "limiting questions" for support in his effort at apologetic theology; see *Whirlwind*, footnote 6, p. 241; also footnote 41, p. 300. The volume referred to is *An Examination of the Place of Reason in Ethics* (Cambridge: Cambridge University Press, 1950). In Chapter 14, "Reason and Faith," pp. 202-21, Toulmin suggests that in secular, logical reasoning a point is reached beyond which one cannot go; he calls such questions "limiting questions." He cautions against mixing modes of reasoning and proposes a logical distinction between "reasons of the heart" and "scientific proofs and reasons" (pp. 216-17). The importance of Toulmin for Gilkey results from the argument that limiting questions are *inevitably* reached as one proceeds to use *secular moral language*. Schubert M. Ogden in his *The Reality of God and Other Essays* (New York: Harper & Row, 1963) makes great use of Toulmin for the same reasons as Gilkey but toward a different theological construction; see pp. 27-39. I am not convinced that Toulmin's argument will bear the freight these contemporary American apologetic theologians

heap upon it. No doubt Toulmin is logically correct that careful examination of moral language eventually uncovers a point of limit. There certainly are questions which cannot be answered (see Toulmin, pp. 209-11), but does this reality of limit provide a foundation for seeking to go beyond limit to give theological answers, as Toulmin suggests (p. 212)? Furthermore, it seems to me that the distinction between matters of fact and logical reason and matters of faith, which Toulmin wishes to draw, assumes an epistemological position which needs to be argued; that is, the sufficiency of man's reason is never questioned. It is not surprising, of course, that Gilkey and Ogden do not raise this objection, for they fall prey to the same assumption.

13. *Whirlwind*, pp. 332-33. Gilkey's argument is, of course, similar to, and dependent upon, the theological achievement of Paul Tillich. The key is Tillich's "method of correlation," as Gilkey notes (see footnote 23, p. 455). He writes: "Two factors are significant in such a theology, one of them a secular question, the other a Christian answer. First of all, in our life in the world, we find that inevitably certain questions, which we have called 'ultimate' questions, arise from our situation as human creatures. ... These quite secular joys and anxieties are the issues with which Christianity has sought to deal. ... Christian faith is, therefore, formally one answer among other possible ones to the questions which secular existence raises for man" (pp. 454-55). See also p. 457.

14. Ibid., 303.

15. Ibid., 182. Gilkey's attempt to move from secular experience to religious affirmation is not unique. Tillich's *Systematic Theology* is most notable among contemporary efforts. Peter Berger has contributed a popular volume growing out of his sophisticated theories of the sociology of knowledge; see *A Rumor of Angels* (Garden City, N.Y.: Doubleday, 1969). David B. Harned's *Grace and Common Life* (Charlottesville, Va.: University Press of Virginia, 1972) proposes that serious examination of key elements of universal common experience may make possible a new effort at cross-cultural theological thought. One of the most interesting recent attempts to move from secular experience to religious reality is Richard R. Niebuhr's *Experiential Religion* (New York: Harper & Row, 1972). Niebuhr finds the present world to be characterized by "the diminished authority of all forms, spheres, and institutions of our life together" (p. 6). The traditional beliefs of the Christian church have no "intrinsic authority" to compel belief (p. 75). Attention to the *affectional life*—experiences such as believing, fear, suffering, and gladness—avoids dogmatic appeal to traditional authority: "The authority we may reasonably look for,

rather, is that of present experience laid open and made readable by a more empirical and less dogmatic view of religion and faith" (p. 48). Niebuhr goes on to argue that man's affectional life may open him to the authority of Jesus in a realization that man's "most authoritative predecessor in such experience was and is Jesus of Nazareth" (p. 106). Such experience seems to point, however, to a power beyond Jesus, to an authority which is "more than Jesus' charisma. It is the authorizing power that augments Jesus" (p. 133). Somehow, the power beyond all human claims energizes and relativizes all mediate authority (p. 113). Niebuhr's book is thoughtful and insightful. It does not, however, adequately deal with the way in which human affectional experience gets one to the point of identifying Jesus as the most authentic predecessor of human experience; suddenly this claim is made without convincing progression (see the confused development on p. 106). Neither is it clear how one is able to recognize the power that augments Jesus without previously experiencing the community of faith which has conserved these symbols (here too Niebuhr's development is confused; i.e., pp. 106, 112-24). Niebuhr is not claiming to do theology; his effort to begin with human experience allows him to achieve an interesting phenomenological analysis of the affections. It appears doubtful that such a method would be useful for theological construction.

16. John B. Cobb, Jr., *Living Options in Protestant Theology: A Survey of Methods* (Philadelphia: Westminster Press, 1962), pp. 316-17; hereinafter referred to as *Living Options*.

17. John B. Cobb, Jr., *God and the World* (Philadelphia: Westminster Press, 1969), pp. 136-37. For the purpose of this section, I am making primary use of *God and the World*; this small volume is an admirably clear statement of Cobb's theological position. Cobb is a prolific writer and has contributed numerous books and articles which come at his Christian natural theology from a number of positions. The most meticulously argued volume of philosophical analysis is his *A Christian Natural Theology: Based on the Thought of Alfred North Whitehead* (Philadelphia: Westminster Press, 1965). See also his article "Speaking About God," *Religion in Life*, XXXVI (Spring 1967), 28-39.

18. From *God and the World*, by John B. Cobb, Jr., p. 138. Copyright © MCMLXIX, The Westminster Press. Used by permission.

19. *Living Options*, p. 313.

20. *God and the World*, p. 138.

21. Ibid., 56.

22. Ibid., 49.

23. Ibid., 55.

24. Ibid., 57.

25. Ibid., 61.

26. *Living Options*, p. 317.

27. Ibid.

28. John B. Cobb, Jr., *The Structure of Christian Existence* (Philadelphia: Westminster Press, 1967), p. 8. See also Cobb's article "From Crisis Theology to the Post-Modern World," *Centennial Review*, VIII (Spring 1964), 184: "Once one enters the strange new world of Whitehead's vision, God becomes very much alive."

29. *The Structure of Christian Existence*, pp. 145-46. See also *God and the World*, p. 130.

30. The method of Cobb's theology is to convince the reader of the soundness of the *philosophical* categories into which theology is translated. This is also the method of Prof. Schubert M. Ogden, of Southern Methodist University. Ogden, too, is dependent on his ability to persuade philosophically. The essence of his natural theology is that examination of man's experience suggests that, in order to live as a self in the world, one must have "an ineradicable confidence in the final worth of our existence" (*The Reality of God and Other Essays* [New York: Harper & Row, 1966], p. 37). By *defining God in terms* of this "ineradicable confidence," Ogden argues that, if understood properly according to his *definition*, every man *must* have faith in God if he is to live in the world. Thus faith in God, for Ogden, is *unavoidable*. He writes: "Faith in God as the ground of confidence in life's ultimate meaning is the necessary condition of our existence as selves" (p. 43). Ogden has won his point, of course, by *definition*; by defining God as he does, he makes faith unavoidable, and therefore meaningless. This method strips theology of meaning by reducing it to elegant philosophical argumentation. The late Daniel Day Williams, of Union Theological Seminary in New York City, in his book *The Spirit and the Forms of Love* (New York: Harper & Row, 1968), has attempted a full-scale systematic theology using the categories of process metaphysics. Like Cobb and Ogden, Williams is also heavily dependent on a Whiteheadian perspective. Williams understands *agape* to be the name for all of God's dealings with men. He traces love in the multiple affairs and actions of man in the world and finds it to be a key to the reality of God. While significantly different from the works of Cobb and Ogden, Williams' argument also depends heavily on definition; that is, God is conceived in terms of aspects of love readily perceivable in a true understanding of the world.

31. Gordon D. Kaufman, *Systematic Theology: A Historicist Perspective* (New York: Charles Scribner's Sons, 1968), p. 116.

32. Ibid., 189.

33. Ibid., 203; see also p. 63.

34. Ibid., xv; also p. 46: "The only decisive question is: Did this event happen or not? Is this historical movement occurring or not? This kind of question can be answered only on the basis of the testimony of appropriate witnesses—submitted, of course, to the most rigorous historical and theological examination to which it can be subjected. In such analysis the objective must be to find out both what the reports declare happened and whether and in what degree they may be taken as veridical."

35. Ibid., 374.

36. Ibid., 375-76; for full account of original sin, see pp. 365-77.

37. See, for instance, *Systematic Theology*, p. 477; Kaufman asserts that the "radicalness of the transvaluation of all human values and conceptions" which Christianity entails "is exposed in all its starkness only when much of the confusing *mythology* of traditional belief, together with the consequent welter of *inconsistent* and *incredible* doctrine, is cut away (as has been attempted in the present work), exposing a powerful unity of fundamental perspective and import." (My emphasis.) See also p. 417; Kaufman insists that accounts of the resurrection must yield to historical interpretation, "otherwise our theology, not being founded on historical actuality, will be agnosticism of speculations and opinions." The meaning of "historical actuality" is that an event can be understood in human terms and judged by human reason.

38. A carefully argued and well-written volume which is of great importance for contemporary theology is Van Austin Harvey's *The Historian and the Believer: The Morality of Historical Knowledge and Christian Belief* (New York: Macmillan, 1966). Harvey's fundamental point is that scientific and historical criticism has provided man with tools by which he can make careful judgments about the adequacy of arguments. This ability has made it morally incumbent upon him to be honest in distinguishing knowledge and belief. This new "ethic of knowledge" is contrasted with an "ethic of belief": "A new ideal of of judgement has gripped the intellect of Western man, and ... this ideal is incompatible with the ethic of belief that has so long been implicit in Christendom" (p. 103). The morality of historical knowledge becomes authoritative for critical appraisal of events and arguments (p. 179). The *reason* of the individual inquirer, submitted only to the morality of historical knowledge, is authoritative; the historian recognizes no external authority: "The historian *confers* authority upon a witness. He reserves the right to judge who or what will be called an authority, and he makes this judgement only after he has

subjected the so-called witness to a rigorous cross-examination" (p. 42). Throughout his work, Harvey's assumption is that man's reason is fully capable of dispassionate, objective evaluation.

39. Gordon D. Kaufman, *God the Problem* (Cambridge, Mass.: Harvard University Press, 1972), p. 24.

40. See *Systematic Theology*, pp. 65-72, for Kaufman's discussion of authority for theological construction; he gives attention to the Bible, the Christian tradition, and the inner conviction of truth (p. 66). Each of these, he concludes, "has been allowed upon occasion to usurp the place belonging rightfully only to the historical event(s) in which God has revealed himself" (p. 71). Kaufman insists that Bible, tradition, and inner conviction are vitally necessary to theology in "threefold reference" (p. 72); nevertheless, functional authority for theology is empirical historical reality. Thomas A. Langford treats this issue in his article "The Historical as Theology's Norm," *Interpretation*, 23 (Oct. 1969), 477-79. Langford notes that Kaufman's "tendency to reduce all theological assertions to what is viable according to a historical method of reasoning detracts from the varied dimensions which theological talk encompasses" (p. 478). He goes on to assert: "It is epistemologically wrong to impose the tight justification required for empirical historical statements upon the whole of theology or to delimit all theological talk to what may be derived from historically verified events" (pp. 478-79).

41. Gordon Kaufman largely accepts Harvey's analysis of the distinction between the morality of historical knowledge and Christian belief. Harvey insists that it is morally wrong to juggle "historical knowledge" to make room for faith. There is no doubt that the historical norm, as he describes it, presents a deeply serious problem for traditional faith. Kaufman agrees with Harvey's analysis, but seeks to demonstrate that it is possible to embrace the morality of historical knowledge *and still* be a man of faith. Harvey is clearly more consistent in his historicism than is Kaufman; he is less willing to grant even the possibility of holding together the norm of historical morality and Christian faith. In *The Historian and the Believer*, Harvey writes: "From liberal Protestantism to the new hermeneutic, Protestant theology may be regarded as a series of salvage operations, attempts to show how one can still believe in Jesus Christ and not violate an ideal of intellectual integrity" (p. 104). It is interesting to note that both Harvey and Kaufman were students of H. Richard Niebuhr at Yale; both demonstrate his influence with regard to interest in the theological problems which result from serious historical research. Niebuhr's own work never resolved the problems of

relativism, but his understanding of the authority of revelation never allowed him to give in to mere historical reason; thus he developed his concept of "internal" versus "external" history in *The Meaning of Revelation*. *Radical Monotheism* was an effort to affirm historical relativism and use it constructively in his treatment of the Absolute reality of the One beyond the many. It may not be incorrect, however, to suggest that Harvey's position is the natural outgrowth of Niebuhr's struggle with historical relativism (which, of course, was an organizing problem for him throughout his career). This view would suggest that Niebuhr too was one among those who participated in the "salvage operations" which sought to demonstrate that one could be historically responsible *and still* a Christian. Niebuhr's brilliant mind and subtle style allowed him to keep the "rough edges" smooth. For Harvey, at least, the "rough edges" became increasingly apparent, and, for *ethical* reasons, he determined that belief does not stand up well in the light of historical reason. On this matter, see also Gordon Kaufman's *Relativism, Knowledge, and Faith* (Chicago: University of Chicago Press, 1960).

42. *Systematic Theology*, footnote 29, pp. 424-25; also p. 431.

43. Ibid., 467. (My emphasis.)

44. Van A. Harvey insists that *morality* demands such precedence: "Indeed, the nineteenth and twentieth centuries have seen the rise of a new phenomenon within the church, the alienated theologian, one who has felt morally compelled to relinquish certain traditional Christian beliefs because he can, in conscience, no longer hold them. No church can afford to ignore this phenomenon: someone who out of love for the truth decides that the church does not represent that truth" (Van A. Harvey, "Secularism, Responsible Belief, and the 'Theology of Hope,'" in *The Future of Hope: Theology as Eschatology*, ed. by Frederick Herzog [New York: Herder & Herder, 1970], p. 133).

45. Jurgen Moltmann, *Theology of Hope* (New York: Harper & Row, 1967). See also Moltmann, *Hope and Planning* (New York: Harper & Row, 1971).

46. Jurgen Moltmann, *The Crucified God* (New York: Harper & Row, 1974).

47. A number of volumes might be mentioned; perhaps especially noteworthy are: Rubem A. Alves, *A Theology of Human Hope* (Washington: Corpus, 1969); Gustavo Gutierrez, *A Theology of Liberation* (Maryknoll, N. Y.: Orbis, 1973); Paulo Freire, *Pedagogy of the Oppressed* (New York: Seabury Press, 1973); and Juan Luis Segundo, *Our Idea of God* (Maryknoll, N.Y.: Orbis, 1974).

48. Letty M. Russell, *Human Liberation in a Feminist Perspective—A Theology* (Philadelphia: Westminster Press, 1974).

49. The women's movement in religion is active on a number of fronts. Heightened consciousness has emphasized the discrimination against women that informs virtually all of the world's religions. One of the functions of religion is the legitimation of roles and values; for this reason, religion has been key to the subordination of women because it has reinforced, rather than challenged, societal assumptions of female inferiority. Any contemporary consideration of women in religion, therefore, must include attention to the historical conditions which gave rise to attitudes about sex roles, to sacred writings which have made them seem eternally valid, to ecclesiastical traditions which have institutionalized them, and to the theological arguments which have justified and perpetuated them.

It is impossible in this book to give attention to these issues. No consideration of contemporary theology can, however, fail to recognize the important theological work which is going on in the women's movement. No one position is representative; a wide range of theological work is being done. Mary Daly, for example, has determined that theology is by definition sexist and therefore her lively and provocative book *Beyond God the Father* is to be understood as philosophy. Daly has written a genuinely radical book. It challenges and rejects all traditional theological methodology and content and asserts the sole authority of women's consciousness. See Mary Daly, *Beyond God the Father: Toward a Philosophy of Women's Liberation* (Boston: Beacon Press, 1973), pp. 6-7. See also Rosemary Radford Ruether, ed., *Religion and Sexism: Images of Woman in the Jewish and Christian Traditions* (New York: Simon and Schuster, 1974), and Alice L. Hageman, ed., *Sexist Religion and Women in the Church: No More Silence* (New York: Association Press, 1974).

50. *Human Liberation in a Feminist Perspective*, pp. 78-80, 135-40.

51. Frederick Herzog, *Liberation Theology: Liberation in the Light of the Fourth Gospel* (New York: Seabury Press, 1972).

52. Ibid., 18. See also Frederick Herzog, *Understanding God: The Key Issue in Present-Day Protestant Thought* (New York: Charles Scribner's Sons, 1966), p. 140: "Our experience of God is still tied to our experience of the Word."

53. *Liberation Theology*, pp. 177, 179.

54. Frederick Herzog, "Introduction: A New Church Conflict?" in *Theology of the Liberating Word*, ed. by Frederick Herzog (Nashville: Abingdon Press, 1971), p. 20.

55. *Liberation Theology*, p. 260. Herzog previously worked out his understanding of hermeneutic and its implications for theological methodology in his book *Understanding God*; see, for instance, pp. 11-15, 103-6.

56. *Liberation Theology*, pp. 2-3.

57. Ibid., 15 and 64.

58. Ibid., 86.

59. See *Liberation Theology*, p. 62: "Jesus revamps Nicodemus' world view. He offers a new idea. What it involves in our day is plain: 'Believe me, no man can see the kingdom of God unless he becomes black' (v. 3)."

60. Ibid., 65.

61. Ibid., 263.

62. James H. Cone, *A Black Theology of Liberation* (Philadelphia: Lippincott, 1970), p. 79.

63. Herzog, in his introduction to *Theology of the Liberating Word* (Nashville: Abingdon Press, 1971), writes: "Just how much is Black Theology repeating the white experience? Who is giving anyone the right to make his experience ultimate authority, regardless of how much on top of the world he feels or how hard pressed he is?" (p. 14). In a footnote on the same page, Herzog writes: "In my opinion, the emergence of black theology is the most important event of the sixties in American theology. An acknowledgement of the achievement, however, does not imply that we should forego critical dialogue."

64. *Liberation Theology*, p. ix.

CHAPTER VI: TOWARD A RECOVERY OF THEOLOGY IN AMERICA

1. From *Naming the Whirlwind: The Renewal of God-Language*, p. 250, copyright © 1969 by Langdon Gilkey, reprinted by permission of the publisher, The Bobbs-Merrill Company, Inc.

2. From *God and the World*, by John B. Cobb, Jr., p. 63. Copyright © MCMLXIX, The Westminster Press. Used by permission.

3. See "From Crisis Theology to the Post-Modern World," *Centennial Review*, VIII (Spring 1964), p. 181: "The Christian thinker today must reach out for a novelty that disdains all appeal to the authority of the past and dares to think creatively and constructively in the present." Also, see Cobb's review of Daniel Day Williams' *The Spirit and the Forms of Love* in *Journal of Religion*, 50 (April 1970), p. 199: "Theologians in the universities no longer care whether they

are 'Christian.' Their norm is much more what makes sense to the ever-changing youth culture than what conforms to the best wisdom of the Christian past." Cobb wrote these words as *descriptive* of the state of contemporary American theology; he noted that Williams' effort is remarkable in that it makes an attempt to account for traditional Christian teachings. Cobb himself accepts as a given that traditional Christian authorities cannot speak to contemporary man; therefore modern theology cannot be dependent on such authority. See *A Christian Natural Theology: Based on the Thought of Alfred North Whitehead*, p. 253: "One's work is theology even if one ignores all earlier statements and begins only with the way things appear to him from that perspective which he acknowledges as given to him in some community of shared life and conviction."

4. In a review of Cobb's *A Christian Natural Theology* in *Theology Today*, 22 (Jan. 1966), 530-45, Langdon Gilkey wrote: "Continually I was forced to ask myself, not so much because of what was said but because all reference to Christian authorities was omitted: 'On what basis does this book call itself a *Christian* natural theology?'—and because of these omissions, I found no satisfactory answer" (p. 531). In a response entitled "Can Natural Theology Be Christian?" also in *Theology Today*, 23 (April 1966), 140-42, Cobb clarifies his intention: "My intention in using the term, however, is to label a particular, and I believe indispensable, *part* of the total task of theology. *This* part of theology must rest its case on philosophical argument, and I believe that this has been the general understanding of natural theology in the past. To appeal to biblical authority in the context of *natural* theology would be to change its character" (p. 140). This does not, however, answer the questions this study is asking of Cobb: What precisely is the authority according to which the theological task proceeds? Is that authority examined and adhered to consistently? What are the implications of that authority for Christian theology? In Cobb's case, these questions must be placed to the philosophical argument, most especially to the claim that a sound philosophical argument is adequate authority for theology.

5. See *God and the World*, p. 63. Schubert M. Ogden shares Cobb's disdain for traditional Christian authorities. This disdain stems from the conviction that secularity has made all such authoritative claims meaningless. Ogden insists, too, that contemporary man's reason must be authoritative for theological construction. See *Christ Without Myth* (New York: Harper & Brothers, 1961), p. 130: "If the price for becoming a faithful follower of Jesus Christ is some form of

self-destruction, whether of the body or of the mind—*sacrificium corporis, sacrificium intellectus*—then there is no alternative but the price remain unpaid."

6. Kaufman, *God the Problem* (Cambridge, Mass.: Harvard University Press, 1972), p. 34.

7. Kaufman, *Systematic Theology* (New York: Charles Scribner's Sons, 1968), p. xii.

8. In a review of Kaufman's *Systematic Theology* in *The Journal of the American Academy of Religion*, 38 (June 1970), 219-21, John B. Cobb, Jr., writes: "I suspect that consistency requires that he become more fully historicist or more fully traditional in his revelational theism" (p. 221).

9. See, for instance, *Liberation Theology* (New York: Seabury Press, 1972), p. 19: "I sought to concentrate on those 'units' of thought that *in my view* bring out the theological significance for today of a particular passage." (My emphasis.) I am only trying to suggest that Herzog *brings to* the scriptures convictions and understandings which help him to interpret them. This is precisely the way it should be, and must be, but it does make the affirmation of biblical authority more complex; thus, the Bible may be authoritative but not *the* authority.

10. Herzog, *Liberation Theology*, p. 196: "But we need to find the outcast and join God there. Otherwise we won't find the church."

11. Ibid., 222.

12. Ibid., 206.

13. Ibid., 195.

14. On this matter see Claude Welch, *Religion in the Undergraduate Curriculum: An Analysis and Interpretation* (Washington, D.C.: Association of American Colleges, 1972), pp. 49-85.

15. An analysis of recent developments in graduate theological education is offered in Claude Welch, *Graduate Education in Religion: A Critical Appraisal* (Missoula, Mont.: University of Montana Press, 1971).

16. William Hamilton, "Thursday's Child: The Theologian Today and Tomorrow," *Theology Today*, XX (Jan. 1964), 491. This essay was reprinted in Thomas J. Altizer and William Hamilton, *Radical Theology and the Death of God* (Indianapolis: Bobbs-Merrill, 1966), pp. 87-93.

17. Van A. Harvey, "Reflections on the Study of Religion," *Journal of the American Academy of Religion*, XXXVIII (March 1970), 21.

18.   Samuel S. Hill, Jr., "Toward a Charter for a Southern Theology," in Samuel S. Hill, Jr., et al., *Religion and the Solid South* (Nashville: Abingdon Press, 1972), p. 181.

19.   *Liberation Theology*, pp. 10-13.

20.   Peter L. Berger and Thomas Luckmann, *The Social Construction of Reality* (Garden City, N.Y.: Doubleday, 1966).

21.   Peter L. Berger, *The Sacred Canopy: Elements of a Sociological Theory of Religion* (Garden City, N.Y.: Doubleday, 1967).

22.   Ibid., 158-59, for example.

23.   Peter L. Berger, "A Call for Authority in the Christian Community," *The Princeton Seminary Bulletin*, LXIV (Dec. 1971), p. 18; see also p. 20.

24.   Ibid., 18.

CHAPTER VII: AUTHORITY FOR THEOLOGY

1.   *North Carolina Christian Advocate*, September 5, 1974, p. 1.

2.   *Living Options*, p. 316.

ABOUT THE AUTHOR

Dennis M. Campbell is a Phi Beta Kappa graduate of Duke University where he received the A.B. degree in 1967. He earned the B.D. degree in 1970 from Yale University where he was William Croft Wilson Scholar. Campbell was named Gurney Harriss Kearns Fellow in Religion at Duke University in 1970 and was awarded the Ph.D. in historical and systematic theology in 1973.

Dr. Campbell is a United Methodist minister and has served parishes in Wisconsin, Connecticut, and North Carolina. He is a member of the North Carolina Conference.

Dr. Campbell is the author of numerous articles and reviews; *Authority and the Renewal of American Theology* is his first book. Since July 1, 1974, Campbell has been assistant professor and chairman of the Department of Religion at Converse College.